Joan Kohn's

it's your kitchen

Joan Kohn's

it's your kitchen

Over 100 Inspirational Kitchens

bulfinch press

AOL TIME WARNER BOOK GROUP

boston • new york • london

First Edition

Library of Congress Cataloging-in-Publication Data
Kohn, Joan.
   Joan Kohn's It's your kitchen : over 100 inspirational kitchens / Joan Kohn —
1st ed. p. cm.
   ISBN 0–8212–2800–5
   1. Kitchens — Design and construction. I. Title.
TX653 .K67 2003
643'.3 — dc21   2002042687

Bulfinch Press is a division of AOL Time Warner Book Group.

Design: Two of Cups Design Studio, Inc.

PRINTED IN SINGAPORE

To Richard, builder of kitchens and bridges,
for his all-enabling vision and love

Acknowledgments

Thanks with all my heart to my dear friends, colleagues, and family members – all of them my teachers – who are so generous and who have contributed in countless ways to this book: to my literary agent, George Greenfield, for reaching out and believing in this project; to Michael Gelick, architect and professor at the University of Illinois at Chicago, for his patient wisdom and extraordinary eye; to writer and producer Marilynn Preston for always inspiring excellence; to Burton Jablon, president of Home & Garden Television, who said yes to the book, to Richard Grant and all my other friends at HGTV, to Peter Finn, executive producer of *Kitchen Design* and *Bed & Bath Design,* to producers Patrice Zabala and John Rice, and special thanks to our first supervising producer, Joyce Richman, who brought me into the HGTV family and contributed so much to the shows; to Paul Leuthe, Tom Kelly, Mick De Giulio, Jamie Drake, Fu-Tung Cheng, Leslie Hart, and Jeff De Mure for setting such high standards for kitchen design; to Linda McClain for her knowledge and encouragement; to Pat Lofthouse for her helpful research; to my fabulous editor at Bulfinch Press, Kristen Schilo, and to Jill Cohen, Karen Murgolo, Eveline Chao, and the whole Bulfinch team for their uncompromising pursuit of quality; to Lisa Vaughn-Soraghan, who designed this beautiful book; to Tom Connors and Judy Hedges for their thoughtful insights on the text; to Richard Kaufman for his definition of clarity; to my wonderful assistant, Taryn Kutchin, for all her energy and creativity throughout this long process; to all the architects and designers whose fine work inspired this book, including those whose work could not be shown here due to limitations of space; to all the photographers whose extraordinary images allow us to see what great ideas look like; and above all, to my husband, Richard, for his tireless support of this project, and to our daughters, Amy and Elizabeth, and our new son Zachary, who sustain us in so many ways.

contents

introduction

When I was seven years old, my parents took me to see Niagara Falls. As we drove slowly down the main street of town, we could see the Falls in the distance, illuminated by a rainbow of colored light. Suddenly I realized that there were tears running down my cheeks, even though I didn't feel at all sad. "Why am I crying?" I asked my mother. "You're crying," she said, "because it's beautiful."

That was my first lesson in the power of beauty. Years later, I learned another lesson: Good design beautifies our lives. In a sense, all of my travels in the world of design — my TV shows, lectures, and personal design projects, and even this book — are extensions of these two simple lessons.

A beautiful environment can inspire us and uplift our spirits. Good design encourages and empowers us. It exhilarates us. It enhances our daily experience. And with it, we provide comfort and refreshment, and make our families feel safe and secure. Incorporating into our lives the elements of good design — such as balance, harmony, and restraint — we remind ourselves of the values by which we wish to live.

Nowhere is this truer than in the kitchen. A well-designed kitchen draws the family together and sets the tone for the day. In recent decades, kitchens have undergone a metamorphosis. Once a merely utilitarian space shut off behind closed doors, the kitchen of today has become the most important room in the house. Functionally and aesthetically, it is the engine and epicenter of the home. Our kitchen doors are not just open — often they are gone altogether, along with the walls. Today's kitchens flow

freely into the dining rooms, home offices, libraries, and playrooms in which we live our hectic, overscheduled, and wonderful lives. And nothing can enhance the look, feel, and function of your home as quickly and dramatically as a new kitchen.

Whether you're building or remodeling, your dream kitchen must be *yours* in every way, reflecting your tastes, your lifestyle, your resources, and most of all your dreams. Whether you hire design professionals or are the captain and crew of your own design team, your kitchen must suit you and not the tastes or expectations of others. Designing a successful kitchen involves making sound, intelligent choices that are right for you.

This book is in two parts. Part one — "Design Essentials" — will help you create a vision for your new kitchen, understand the basic elements of kitchen design, assess your existing kitchen, budget your resources, gather inspiration, choose your design style, and assemble and work with a design team. In part two — "The Five Building Blocks of Kitchen Design" — the critical design choices involved in five fundamental areas of kitchen design are addressed: function, space, floor plan, style, and *you*, enabling you to turn your kitchen vision into reality.

It's Your Kitchen is filled with gorgeous kitchens designed by top architects and kitchen designers, and covers a wide array of traditional and contemporary design styles, each chosen to represent kitchen design at its very best. They are intended to spark your imagination and provide useful ideas to help you make design choices effortlessly and with confidence.

10 (prelude)

prelude: pantry of the sun

In this quiet moment before we step into the kitchen, let's linger briefly in this *Pantry du Soleil* (opposite), created by designer Mick De Giulio.

Once a modest servant's kitchen, and now a passage connecting a new kitchen with the dining room and library, this pure cube evokes a templelike serenity, the perfect place for contemplating kitchens.

There is a balance here, between old and new, between light and shadow, between that which is revealed and that which is concealed. There is clarity as well as mystery. In many ways, the graceful oppositions in this simple pantry tell the story of kitchen design today.

Kitchens were once secondary spaces. In grand houses, they were seen only by servants. In more humble homes, they were often cramped and inefficient — a space guests were never meant to see. But today, kitchens are the busiest and most beautiful rooms in the home, the rooms in which we invest the most time and energy . . . so much of ourselves.

Now we enter our kitchens through the *front* door, and sometimes through refined spaces such as the pantry shown here. We show respect for the commitment we have made to live beautiful, productive lives by building kitchens in which aesthetic issues are as rigorously valued as any sink, stove, or refrigerator. This pantry began with the designer's vision of an elegant, organic flow of open space. Because it is an interior room with no source of natural light, De Giulio created a sense of light pouring in through clerestory windows by painting the illuminated interiors of the uppermost clear-glass cabinets a luminous cornflower blue. With sanded glass below, the illusion of a bright sky is completed as "sun" streams in from above.

"Wrinkled and dirty" doors from an old library (found, then saved for seven years) relax and humanize the crisp, quarter-note rhythms of the four-by-four sets of two-over-two glazed door panels, the knobs in groups of four, and the double sets of four drawers below.

The cabinets come to rest 6" below the ceiling, allowing the architecture of the space to express itself. And, in a shape that mirrors the architecture, a square sisal mat on the floor adds a solid plane of texture over the 18" x 24" variegated limestone slabs set in a running bond pattern.

The austerity of the pantry is softened by an arched portal and a subtle radius on the steps to the landing. Then in perfect equipoise, center stage, beneath her own alabaster light, a pale, ash entry table rests on gently curving legs.

With its elegant blend of lessons from both traditional and modern design, this "Pantry of the Sun" welcomes us all into today's kitchen.

part one:

design essentials

Every beautiful kitchen begins with a vivid dream. Let your imagination soar!

ABOVE AND OPPOSITE Two personal visions — one inspired by the granite bridge, pond, and woods outside, the other by the elegant European style of the adjoining rooms.
Design: Thomas Richard Kelly [above], Deborah T. Lipner [opposite]

every kitchen has a personality. How do you see yours? Is it a quiet, gentle room or an opinionated space with a bit of attitude? Is it nostalgic or forward-looking? Has this kitchen been traveling to Italy, Japan, France, or Morocco? Does it like to party or does it prefer to be alone with a cup of tea and a good book? Does it wear denim or silk? Does it let you lean back and kick off your shoes or make you sit up straight? Is this a kitchen you can really talk to or does it demand your "best behavior"? Is your new kitchen a generous room that will pay you back for all the time and effort you put into planning it, or will it continually demand more time and effort? Will this room be sensitive to you and everyone else in your family? Will it support who you are today and the person that you are becoming? Will this new design be fun to live with?

one

vision

Like an Olympic runner who visualizes herself crossing the finish line in record time; a chef who knows exactly how a dish will taste even before it's finished; or the acclaimed architect Frank Lloyd Wright, who completed his drawings in his mind before pencil ever met paper, you must have a clear vision of your new kitchen before you build it — a vision to excite and inspire you, to guide you through the many design choices that will confront you along the way, and to sustain you when you're ankle-deep in plaster dust.

Arriving at that vision is a two-step process. Step one is to dream, no matter how fantastically. Step two is to interpret those dreams, refining them in light of more practical considerations, such as the square footage and configuration of your available space, your specific functional needs, and your resources. Like a string on a kite, each consideration will help you hold on to your dream and prevent it from soaring out of sight. When this second step is completed, you will have a highly evolved and detailed concept of how your new kitchen will look and function.

Generating a kitchen vision should be a fluid process, evolving as new ideas spark your imagination. You may begin with a fixed concept of how you want your kitchen to look, but once you immerse yourself in the design process, your ideas may change. This can be especially true when remodeling an existing kitchen. It could be that the wall you planned to tear down turns out to be load bearing and will have to stay, or that you ripped out a dropped soffit only to discover it conceals plumbing for the apartment upstairs. Be prepared for such unexpected discoveries, and welcome them as opportunities to unleash your creative energies. In a way, they are gifts.

ABOVE This robust, inviting kitchen is designed to satisfy lots of hungry guests. Commercial cooking equipment; a heavy-duty, steel pot rack with integrated lighting; and a very serious stainless service island are balanced with softer, homier details such as warm, maple flooring and simple Shaker-style cabinets.
Design: Chip Webster

OPPOSITE Sculpted from abstract geometric forms and indirect lighting, this kitchen quietly expresses a vision of the power of simplicity. In a refined palette of wheat-colored maple wood and black granite, the space gracefully opens to join the adjacent living and dining areas, declaring that today's kitchen is clearly as important and as beautiful as any other room in the home.
Design: Brininstool + Lynch

OPPOSITE Keeping Hawaiian heritage alive while incorporating the home owner's personal style was the vision behind this kitchen renovation in a colonial plantation-style home in Manoa, on the island of Oahu.
Design: Troy L. Adams

RIGHT Created with daring vision and a few bold architectural strokes, this kitchen, walled with windows, sits under a canopy of galvanized steel that seems to float among the surrounding treetops on ten acres of lush countryside, giving the entire space a feeling of serenity. The warmth of natural maple wood, pewter soapstone, and a marble conglomerate further enhance the strength of this design.
Design: Sura Malaga-Strachan

Step One: Spinning Kitchen Dreams

There are only a few rules to keep in mind when conjuring up kitchen dreams:

First, they must be *your* dreams — not your friend's, not your decorator's, and not even your mother's. It can be important to consider the views of others. Input from family members can be invaluable. But fundamentally, it's your kitchen, and the dreams it reflects must be yours.

Second, your dreams should be sweet. The creative process demands flights of fancy, so *dream wide* and *dream big!* Don't edit your imagination. Even bad ideas have their place. I know one designer who always asks new clients to bring in a list of what they love, and what they don't. Ask yourself, "What

kitchen would I design if I were not afraid of making a mistake, or had no budgetary constraints?" Push the limits of your personal rules of order and design. Dare to consider the unexpected, and even the impossible. Indulge in free association. Remember, ideas pop up for a reason. Your creative brain has a powerful, built-in logic; learn to trust it. Don't restrict yourself by what you have known or done in the past. At this point, the only consideration is what makes you smile.

Third, don't rush the process. Schedules, alarms, and deadlines come later. For now, take your time. Going slowly may seem like an indulgence, but it is actually a wise investment that will pay you back with big dividends. The more specifically and deliberately you plan today, the clearer and better your kitchen vision will be.

LEFT AND OPPOSITE   A vivacious
blending of past, present, and future
makes this a vision that delights the eye.
Design: Jackie Brown and Marc-Michaels
Interior Design, Inc.

Step Two: Interpreting Your Kitchen Dreams

Once you have collected your kitchen dreams, you can begin
to interpret them — to *refine* them by making adjustments and
revisions that are just right for you. Balancing your design
fantasies with your realities will give you a sustainable
vision — the perfect blueprint for success.

Ask yourself these questions:

➤ How can my dream be realized in the space available? Will I
   have to break down walls, punch holes for new windows, add
   skylights, or make other major architectural adjustments?
   Will I have to modify existing traffic patterns in my home?

➤ Does my dream fit my budget? If not, don't despair. Even
   though you may not be able to re-create the kitchen you
   saw in your favorite design magazine, you may be able to
   capture the essence of it in an affordable way by adopting
   the same color palette, or including just a few of its key
   elements in your kitchen design. Or you may be able to
   realize your dream in stages, perhaps using plastic laminate
   countertops now and upgrading to another material later.

➤ How does my dream kitchen fit into the decor and scale
   of the rest of my home?

➤ Are there appliances or other elements of my existing
   kitchen that I wish to recycle into my new kitchen?

➤ How will my dream kitchen affect my home's resale value?

Refining your dream can be as exciting as the dream itself.
Although this process almost always involves some adjustments, that doesn't mean that the dream itself will be lost. On
the contrary, thoughtful adjustments can enhance your kitchen
design. Think about how you can extract the *essence* of your
dream — the core ideas that will have the most impact, even
on a modest scale.

If your kitchen dreams are not yet fully formed,
there are many ways to stimulate your imagination. One
obvious way is to collect pictures from magazines and
books — not to mention your favorite TV shows! — using the
techniques discussed in chapter five. Or perhaps the kitchen
seating areas assembled in chapter six will help you to recognize your kitchen dream when you feel it.

But there are other great ways to spark your imagination:

➤ Analyze precisely why you want a new kitchen, and how
   you want to use it. You'll find checklists to help you along
   with this process in chapter eight.

➤ Decide what you like, and what you do not like, about
   your existing kitchen, and interview your family members
   to get their thoughts.

➤ Through it all, keep a detailed written wish list chroni-
   cling your observations as they occur to you.

ABOVE, RIGHT, AND OPPOSITE
This late Victorian kitchen vision takes us back to the turn of the last century to create an all-embracing sense of time gone by. By taking design cues from the original architecture of the 1887 home, using authentic materials and fixtures, and camouflaging modern appliances behind period-style cabinetry, the designer has created a perfect picture.
Design: Jean Stoffer

Kitchen dreams may take many forms:

➤ **Your dreams may be about** *food* — the heavy aroma of chocolate-chip-cookie dough in a large mixing bowl, luring family members into the kitchen; the smell and sound of onions and garlic sizzling in an open fry pan; or an image of yourself . . . alone with the newspaper and a cup of coffee early in the morning.

➤ **Your dreams may be about** *function* — how you see yourself using your new kitchen. Are you a gourmet chef seeking the best-equipped stage on which to act out your culinary fantasies? Or a retiree looking for a quiet sanctuary in which to greet each precious new day?

 Do you envision yourself cooking with friends and family gathered around? Or are you a fast-track urbanite who wants a sleek, granite countertop on which to lay out cartons of carryout food? Do you see your kitchen as "command central," where a telephone and computer are as important as a stove and sink? Perhaps you use a wheelchair and long for a kitchen that graciously accommodates your individual needs.

➤ **Your dreams may be about** *style* — French country, Early American, Tuscan, Victorian, modern, or an eclectic combination.

➤ **Your dreams may be as simple as a** *memory* — of long conversations at your grandmother's kitchen table when you were a child, of the bustle and laughter that signal the preparation of a holiday meal, or of the warmth of a stone fireplace in a bed-and-breakfast you visited one winter weekend. Your new kitchen can evoke that memory every day.

➤ **Your dreams may be about** *color* — you may have always imagined yourself in a classic white English kitchen, or yearned to "go retro" with pink and turquoise. Perhaps you just want to surround yourself with your favorite color. The kitchen is a perfect place in which to do just that.

➤ **Your dreams may be about creating an** *emotional impact* — a sense of serenity, drama, or surprise.

➤ **Your dreams may be about** *light* — you may envision yourself standing at the sink in front of a picture window as the morning sun pours in, or as dusk settles.

➤ **Your dreams may be about** *space* — breaking down existing walls to borrow space from adjacent hallways, closets, or other rooms to create a sense of openness. This was the dream that inspired my own kitchen in Chicago.

➤ **Your dreams may be about** *your future* — your life as you wish it to become. Design can move us emotionally, but it can also move us in a more literal sense, by inspiring and enabling us. I have a friend who built a small photography darkroom in an old pantry as a way of jumpstarting the hobby she had always dreamed of. In this way, design can be a catalyst for change in our lives.

➤ **Your dreams may be about having a kitchen that is** *original,* a kitchen no one else has — uniqueness as an end in itself.

A Word about Resale

Because the kitchen has become so central to our lives and such a significant element of home design, you may wish to remodel your kitchen solely to make your home more marketable. But beware! This strategy can backfire in a surprising yet pleasant way. I have heard many stories from home owners who remodeled their kitchens for resale, only to fall in love with their new kitchens and decide not to move! There is also the risk that, by the time you decide to sell, market tastes may have shifted.

I am convinced that if you design just for yourself, the power and integrity of your vision will draw the right buyer to your home. I love the story told to me by an antiques dealer who owned a boutique specializing in French imports. The decor of her shop incorporated strong colors borrowed from a traditional French country palette, including walls painted

LEFT AND BELOW A faux skylight reveals the antique beams above this one-of-a-kind kitchen vision.
Design: Emanuela Frattini Magnusson

forest green. She loved these colors so much that she used them in her kitchen. But when she decided to sell her home, she had difficulty finding a realtor willing to take on the assignment; they all insisted that she first paint her kitchen walls white! Finally, she found a broker, but for the longest time no prospective buyers appeared. Then one day, a young couple came to see the house and immediately fell in love with it. "I don't believe it!" exclaimed the excited young woman to her husband. "This house looks just like that French antiques store we love so much!"

There is also the Paris couple who cooked at home so infrequently that they did not want their new loft apartment to have any kitchen at all. Convinced by their designer that a kitchen of some kind was an absolute necessity, they opted for one that sat in the space like a piece of sculpture. The striking result is the kitchen shown opposite.

LEFT AND OPPOSITE There is
drama in this kitchen vision,
concealed yet slyly revealed by
a towering wall that seems to float
in space.
Design: Ruhl Walker Architects

Final Thoughts

It should be apparent by now that developing your kitchen vision is a dynamic process that can yield unexpected and wonderful results. Once you have your vision in place, it will help you to navigate the sea of design choices that lies ahead, making the journey easier and all the more enjoyable.

Furthermore, once you've begun construction, having a clear vision can give you the strength and focus to complete the project. When your painter's truck has broken down for the third time, and when the only sink in your kitchen is the feeling in the pit of your stomach, your vision will keep you going. I learned this lesson years ago from my husband, Richard, during our first kitchen remodeling project. Whenever I began to panic, he reassured me by reminding me of how beautiful our new kitchen would be. He had a clear vision. He could actually see the kitchen as it would ultimately turn out! Eventually, I learned to trust that vision and to allow myself to accept the uncertainty and stress inherent in the messy construction process.

Finally, having tapped into your imagination to create your kitchen vision, you're likely to find yourself approaching the rest of your life more creatively.

One of the unexpected joys of designing a new kitchen is that you begin to see and think like an artist.

ABOVE AND OPPOSITE Behind a sliding wall of fire-etched glass, pure geometry and function unite in this mirror-finished kitchen composition.
Design: Abramson Teiger Architects

every beautiful kitchen is a three-dimensional work of art and architecture. While on the surface of the room we see cabinets, countertops, and sinks, by stepping back a bit and squinting our eyes the way artists do when they are analyzing a painting, we see that kitchens, like all compositions, are made up of a few basic design elements.

Some of these elements, such as line, texture, color, and mass, have physical dimensions. Others, such as harmony, clarity, and restraint, are more abstract. But together, these individual elements make up the basic vocabulary that is written into every good design.

Developing an easy familiarity with these fundamental concepts helps us to make good design decisions, and allows us to communicate our kitchen visions with greater accuracy.

two

the elements of kitchen design

Line

Lines can be straight or curved, short or long, wide or narrow. It is the infinite variety of ways in which they can be repeated or broken, ornamented or simplified, that gives this element of design the power to define the style of your kitchen.

Line also conveys emotion. Thick lines suggest strength. Thin lines imply delicacy. Angled lines can be energetic. Lines can be brash or passive, subtle or bold, sturdy or ephemeral.

Like lines of music, the lines of a kitchen combine to create unique rhythms and patterns. Some kitchens have smooth lines that seem to waltz while others have lines that cha-cha-cha or really rock and roll. Some lines whisper and some lines shout.

Generally, traditional styles are characterized by more curved and ornamented lines while contemporary styles tend to employ straighter, less-embellished lines.

ABOVE AND OPPOSITE Line has the power to define the style of your kitchen.
Design: Brininstool + Lynch [above], Sandra L. Steiner [opposite]

Texture

The most sensual element of design is texture, because it appeals to our tactile as well as visual senses. The textures we feel also act upon our emotions and make *us* feel. Sleek, sophisticated textures can cool down a design. Richly woven textures can warm it up.

Every material has texture. By juxtaposing rough surfaces against smooth, hard against soft, heavy against delicate, natural against synthetic, patterned against plain, and reflective against matte, we can enliven a design with visual interest and variety.

Because it is an innate part of every material we choose, texture can enter the kitchen in unobtrusive ways: shiny stainless steel; grained butcher block; dappled granite; porous concrete; mottled copper; patterned laminates; glossy enamel; fibrous bamboo; fused, pressed, ribbed, or etched glass; silk, canvas, or chenille.

Without attracting direct attention to itself, texture can have a quiet but critical impact on a design, and when its potential is ignited, it can boldly take charge of a kitchen's look.

OPPOSITE AND ABOVE Texture can enter the kitchen in unobtrusive ways.
Design: Strittmatter Studios [opposite], Cameron Snyder [above]

LEFT The most sensual element of design is texture, because it appeals to our tactile as well as visual senses.
Design: Dalia Tamari

Color

Color may be the central theme of a kitchen or may quietly serve to support and enhance other elements of your design. Either way, every design decision you make is a color decision too. Neutrals are not necessarily neutral in terms of their impact on your design, and even white is very much a color in the kitchen. Each material you select, including natural stones and metals, carries its own hue. So whether it's a matte-finished taupe or a glossy fire-engine red, color demands close attention in every phase of kitchen design.

More than any other element of design, color is emotion. It will determine and dominate the mood of your kitchen decor.

Most of us feel at home with color; after all, we begin playing with colors when we get our first box of crayons. We all have a favorite color, and a color we love to hate. But in kitchen design, even simple color can quickly become complex. Color can be opaque or transparent; warm or cool;

tinted or shaded; saturated or diluted; iridescent, metallic, reflective, or flat; milky or grayed-down. Colors change with the light and appear different on different surfaces. New technologies produce colors with chameleonlike properties — colors that are layered, holographic, and magical.

Because each of us has deeply intuitive reactions to color, you are your own best color expert. Observe your color responses and then respect your instinct.

OPPOSITE More than any other element of design, color is emotion.
Design: Woodmeister Corp.

ABOVE LEFT In kitchen design, even simple color can quickly become complex.
Design: Emanuela Frattini Magnusson

ABOVE RIGHT Color can be opaque or transparent; warm or cool; tinted or shaded; saturated or diluted; iridescent, metallic, reflective, or flat; milky or grayed-down.
Design: Adolfo Perez

Mass

While you can draw a perfect kitchen picture using lines, textures, and colors, to build a kitchen you must put on your 3-D glasses. Mass begins with line, which then moves into space — collecting heft, depth, and height. One rectangle drawn on paper will become a refrigerator in your new kitchen; another will be transformed into a center island where you will prepare food, wash dishes, and eat your breakfast.

Kitchens are high-performance sculptures that must be evaluated both aesthetically and physically for the sake of practicality, comfort, and beauty. Therefore, as you visualize your new design, walk yourself through all its spaces. A stove, refrigerator, cabinet, island, table, and almost anything else that fills a kitchen has mass. Negative space is the emptiness between the elements — all the recesses, nooks, and corridors. When sculpting your kitchen, your goal should be to find the balance between positive masses and negative spaces.

Because life in the kitchen means constant physical inter-action with large appliances and massive architectural constructs, kitchen forms must be measured with the body as well as the eye, and every form must fit its function — and its owners — for any aesthetic to be truly pleasing.

RIGHT Mass begins with line, which then moves into space — collecting heft, depth, and height.
Design: Colette and William Rodon Hornof

LEFT Kitchens are high-performance sculptures.
Design: Fu-Tung Cheng

Scale

Composing a kitchen design is a delicate process of finding the proper relationship of each piece to every other piece, as well as the proper relationship of each piece to the whole.

The kitchen itself must be properly sized in relationship to the home and all the adjoining spaces. Separate areas within the kitchen must be proportioned, and, of course, all the individual pieces inside must work well together.

Improper proportions can sabotage even the most well-conceived kitchen design whereas good proportion often exerts its power anonymously, and may go unnoticed.

Harmony + Contrast = Balance

In good design, line, color, texture, and form blend together gracefully, allowing the whole composition to "set." There must also be enough visual variety, however, to keep a design from becoming boring or monotonous. Such contrast can be achieved through bold juxtapositions of elements, or with gentle understatement.

Balance is the hallmark and key, the single most important measure of good design work.

Yet there is still a bit more to be said. Designs that rise above "successful" to reach the realm of greatness include two more elements.

ABOVE Good proportion often exerts its power anonymously, and may go unnoticed.
Design: Foster Dale

OPPOSITE Balance is the hallmark and key, the single most important measure of good design work.
Design: Andre Rothblatt

Clarity

Clarity is honesty delivered with directness.

At the center of your home, your kitchen can tell whatever story you want in the lovely, wordless language of color, texture, and form.

Yours may be a story about food or family and friends, a story about serenity or hard work. Your design may focus on sustaining a healthy planet or traveling around the planet.

The truer it is to who you are and the values you cherish, the more powerful — and the more interesting — it will be. Whether your style is plain or fancy, classic or of your own invention, put authenticity into every choice you make.

Restraint

For aspiring artists, one of the most difficult lessons to learn is when to stop working on a painting. Overworking a piece will quickly muddy all the beautiful colors and forms.

If water is already boiling, turning up the heat won't make it any hotter; it only causes the water to evaporate, and you end up with less. Knowing when to stop adding to a kitchen design is precisely the same. Once your kitchen is beautiful, let it be.

ABOVE Clarity is honesty delivered with directness.
Design: Andre Rothblatt

OPPOSITE Once your kitchen is beautiful, let it be.
Design: Sally Cernik Weston

Final Thoughts

It's not easy to describe the magic we feel watching a flickering bonfire, or the way beautiful music thrills us. But we know what it takes to get a flame going, and how much training and discipline it must take to sing an aria by Mozart.

Great design is also magical and thrilling. We may not have words to describe the exhilaration we feel when we encounter it, but once we understand the fundamental elements of design, we have a much better idea of how to achieve it.

When handled adeptly, these elements of kitchen design work together in subtle ways. They don't call attention to themselves, but simply give a kitchen that sense of "rightness" we all strive for.

Your present kitchen holds the keys
to your future design success.

S tarting over does not necessarily mean starting from scratch. Constructive analysis of your existing kitchen will help you decide "what must stay" and "what must go," providing you with essential design clues for your next kitchen.

This chapter includes a tool kit for maximizing your creativity, self-knowledge, and powers of observation; a questionnaire; and a before-and-after story of a remodeling project that sensitively restored an old kitchen and added just the right twist of modernity.

three

assessing your existing kitchen

Joan's Tool Kit

Most toolboxes are filled with screwdrivers, hammers, pliers, and an array of screws and nails. But the kit you will need to complete your kitchen design includes different tools: those necessary to harness your creativity, honest self-awareness, and skills of observation and communication. These tools will help you solve problems and deal with challenges and frustrations as they come up — or maybe even before they do. The contents of this kit are described below, with instructions for getting the most out of each tool.

For order and convenience, keep your tools together in one place. A nylon-mesh gardening bag, a plumber's satchel, a basket, or a tote bag of any kind will work. Set the right standard for your kitchen-design project by choosing a container that is as pleasant to look at and touch as it is convenient to use. Then fill it with these basic tools:

Camera

Find the lightest and most compact camera you can, one that will be easy to carry wherever you go. Good ideas are found in unusual and surprising places. Your camera eliminates the pressure of remembering massive amounts of information. While you may be able to retain a general sense of the stonework in the kitchen of that bed-and-breakfast you stayed at last summer, your camera will capture all the minute details — critical information that can make a huge design difference in your new kitchen.

Your camera can also help you to become an effective detective during the assessment and evaluation stage of your remodeling project. By employing the impartial lens of your camera, you can observe with greater objectivity the realities of your room, and make judicious and economical decisions about what to save and recycle into your new design, and what to eliminate. If you are wondering what the camera can see that you can't, the answer is *plenty*. Unlike you, your camera doesn't see only what it wants to see. It can't ignore that ragtag nest of knotted wires on the countertop, skim lightly over the cracked and peeling plaster above the cabinets, or block out the unsightly stains on the old linoleum flooring. By using your camera's eye, you will eventually train your own eyes to be more objective too. The lessons your camera can teach you will help you become more discerning and improve your ability to edit the choices you make.

Tape Recorder

While a camera will help you *see* your existing kitchen with more clarity, your tape recorder is about *listening*. It is included in your tool kit to help you tune in to the needs of the people with whom you will share your new kitchen. If your camera turned you into a detective, then your tape recorder will make you a journalist. Interview all the members of your family, giving them the time they need to answer the questions that you have already asked yourself (using the questionnaire on pages 48–49). The conversations you save will have a significant impact on your vision and will help you create a kitchen that serves the needs of all the people you love best.

Listening, like seeing, can easily become a selective process. It is always easier to hear what we want to hear than it is to really listen. In the long run, careful listening pays off. It ultimately simplifies the process of making choices because it limits your range of options. For example, if Mom has her heart set on a warm and sunny color scheme, Dad says no to floral prints, and the kids insist on something funky, selecting seat cushions for the kitchen chairs becomes simpler because you've already narrowed your focus. When everybody agrees on a bright-yellow plaid, you'll be happy you listened to your family's opinions.

Yellow Sticky Notes

These little guys can be a big help, assisting you in preparing a precise wish list of changes based on the reality of your current design problems and how you live meal-to-meal and day-to-day. Using them couldn't be simpler. Every time you notice a design flaw in your existing kitchen, take a moment to jot it on a sticky note and then paste that note directly onto the offending spot. Is that junk drawer too hard to open? Mark it yellow. Does the pantry door open in the wrong direction, interrupting the traffic pattern in the kitchen? Slap on a sticky. That slow leak under the sink? Give it the yellow badge of discouragement too. Once your kitchen looks like a lemon, you'll know it's time to remodel.

Measuring Tape

To insure that all your good ideas fit into your new room, include a tape measure in your tool kit. Proper proportions and a good fit are necessary from floor to ceiling and all around your kitchen layout. Professional carpenters always say "Measure twice, cut once." It's a good rule to follow as you connect all the pieces of your kitchen-design puzzle, whether you are shopping for appliances, planning your cabinetry, arranging the seating area, or making decisions about how best to use the empty space under the staircase. No part of kitchen design should be a guessing game. If in doubt, measure three times.

Calendar / Address Book

Keeping your paperwork accurate and orderly is a must. Even more important is keeping an organized list of correct names, addresses, fax numbers, e-mail addresses, and telephone numbers. A higher priority still is getting to know the people you are working with, understanding their work habits, and finding convenient and comfortable ways to communicate with them.

Unless you have a photographic memory or are a social genius, you will need to write down the details. Write them *all* down. Do your best to address everyone by name — not just your contractor, painter, or the head salesperson at your favorite appliance store, but assistants, part-timers, and helpers as well. People are put at ease when you use their names — it's a gracious first step toward establishing good relationships.

The calendar is important for scheduling work, arranging deliveries, and keeping appointments. It's also the best place to maintain a running list of the agreements and arrangements that you've made with workmen and others. Daily jottings on your calendar, including names and specific notes about conversations and promises made, are a practical and easy way to keep chaos and mental confusion to a minimum.

Receipts File

A folder dedicated for your receipts and bills will help you monitor and assess the many financial aspects of your kitchen project. Knowing where you stand financially is crucial to completing your job in the style (both yours and your kitchen's) in which you began it. No matter how luxurious your new kitchen may be, you won't get unqualified pleasure from it if you have gone uncomfortably overbudget. Balance is the hallmark of all great designs — financially as well as aesthetically.

Hand Mirror

Self-knowledge is the key to design success. Use this tool to look yourself squarely in the eye. It will help you answer honestly all the questions in the preparatory questionnaire that follows, enable you to set appropriate design goals, and aid you in making choices throughout your project. While you may not employ this most important tool often, please take its value seriously enough to include it in your tool kit. It will serve as a reminder of how crucial it is to know yourself as you design and build your kitchen.

Journal

Designing and building a new kitchen is a big deal! It will monopolize your time, energy, creativity, right brain, left brain, and virtually all your resources for a long time. A good way to collect your thoughts (and yourself!) is to keep a journal. As the head of your design team, you should consider following the example of artists and leaders in all fields who have employed with great success this time-tested method of self-exploration and discovery. A fifteen-minute investment every day (for me, morning is best) will pay you back with more than just a few short pages of penmanship practice. A journal is like a new best friend: It is happy to hear all your excitement and complaints, and it can provide you with wonderful new insights about yourself. In it you can record new ideas, express your joys, vent your tensions and fears, and grapple with your problems. You don't have to be right or wrong. You can babble. You can brag. Whining is okay too. See my journal entry in chapter seven.

cabinetry on the adjoining wall over the hearth. Task lights built into the soffit illuminate the concrete countertop and impart a sense of architectural permanence to the design. The glazed doors that frame the microwave oven (now happily off the countertop) add variety and depth to the room.

The new stainless refrigerator fits neatly under an upper cabinet that was custom designed with pivot doors, hiding a television set. Bead-board detailing on the cabinetry by the sink (echoing the bead board of the bookcases) joins with the concrete countertops and backsplashes to add more subtle textural variation.

New features, including a hot-water tap, soap dispenser, and the shallow refrigerator, are finished in stainless steel, chosen for its simple neutrality. The concrete (not an obvious choice) was an artful touch suggested by the designer, who knew that its earthy, barely celadon tint and flat finish would complement Jackie's pottery and art collections. The walls also take on a slight green cast, and as a finishing touch, Jackie's favorite vintage poster hangs above the sink.

Before . . . and After

Having lived in her vintage city home for several years, Jackie Leimer had a head start on remodeling because she really knew her kitchen and herself. Taking design cues from the Victorian home's exterior architecture and interior millwork, she wanted to restore a sense of authenticity to this kitchen within its original footprint while modernizing the design to suit her current needs.

According to Jackie, the floor plan was a bit quirky, but since she'd already become accustomed to working between the two opposing L-shaped counters, she decided not to alter the basic layout. There were several problems, however, that did need solving.

The cabinetry was definitely high on that list. The lack of adequate storage space had turned the counters into catchalls for clutter. Sensitive to the dimensions and details of the original hutch just a step down the corridor, designer Ashley Cole gave the new cabinetry an old-style refinement and delicacy that blends seamlessly into this space (right and opposite).

The old, protruding soffit that they "couldn't get rid of" because it housed pipes became one of those wonderful opportunities that arises from an architectural problem. They decided to clad it with inset panels and finish it with crown molding that would flow seamlessly and elegantly into the

Assessing Your Kitchen Needs

Here's a questionnaire to help focus your thoughts on how you want your new kitchen to look and feel:

Part A. Lifestyle and Aesthetics

1. On a scale of 1–10, how beautiful is your existing kitchen?

2. On a scale of 1–10, how well does it work for you?

3. How often do you find yourself yearning to replace an old appliance or worn countertop, or to change your kitchen in some other way?

4. How have your kitchen needs changed in recent years? Do you spend more time in the kitchen now, or less?

5. How many people use the kitchen every day?

6. How many cooks do you have in your household?

7. How many meals a week do you eat at home?

8. Do you have a favorite spot in the kitchen? What makes it your favorite?

9. What parts of your kitchen are "must-haves" in your next design?

10. What can you live without? Is there something about your kitchen design that annoys you on a regular basis? Something that causes a constant struggle, or that makes you say to yourself, "I'll have to fix that someday"?

11. What's your visceral reaction as you enter your kitchen? Does the room draw you in and comfort you?

12. Does your design accommodate every member of the family? Is there room for everyone to be comfortable, and ample storage for each individual's needs?

13. Are your family pets "at home" in the kitchen? Is there a convenient spot for their food dishes and toys?

14. How do you feel when you are alone in your kitchen? Are you content? Do you find yourself spending as much time as possible there? Is there a sense that something is missing or that the room is overcrowded?

15. Rank the rooms in your house in order of preference. How high on the list is your kitchen? What characteristics about your favorite room might you bring into your new design?

16. How well does your kitchen work when you are entertaining? Do you have room to cook and room for guests to gather?

17. Are you at ease when friends come into your kitchen, or do you want to whisk them out into other areas of your home?

18. Is your kitchen wired for current and future communication, entertainment, and other technical needs?

Part B. Space

1. Do you have enough space for all your kitchen activities? Is your kitchen too big? Too small?

2. How's the traffic pattern? Do you and others have ample room to move around and through the kitchen with ease?

3. Do you find yourself bumping into objects or people?

4. Have you noticed any recurrent annoyances, such as having to walk around the island to get to your sink, or eye strain as you chop vegetables on a poorly lit surface?

5. Do you have to walk too far between kitchen tasks?

6. How is the view from the sink?

7. Do you have comfortable seating for yourself and others? Would you like the option of sitting as you work?

8. How's the traffic flow between your kitchen and the adjacent rooms?

9. How well does your kitchen relate to the out-of-doors? Is the exterior door well situated? Do you have a practical transition between the outside and inside? Is there a mudroom or closet near the back door? Would a utility sink or powder room improve the space?

10. How convenient is it for you to recycle or take out the trash?

Part C. Storage

1. Is unpacking your groceries an orderly procedure, or do you feel scattered and confused? Are your cold and dry storage areas in close proximity? Do you have a convenient spot for the grocery bags you are unloading?

2. Can you find what you need, when you need it, in the kitchen, or do you have to rummage and hunt?

3. Do you, when cleaning out your cupboards, find things that you didn't know you still had?

4. Are condiments, spices, and utensils within easy reach when you cook?

5. Do you have room to display your decorative pieces and art? Are they well illuminated?

6. Are there hidden opportunities for storage, such as empty corners or an unused area under a stairwell?

7. Have you stored things in the attic or basement that you wish you could be using regularly?

8. Are your cupboards filled with items you never use?

9. If you had more storage space, what would be the first thing that you'd put there?

Part D. Condition

1. What is the current condition of your kitchen — floors, ceilings, cabinet finishes, countertops, walls, and trim?

2. Are your appliances in good working order? Do they match your current cooking habits?

3. Are your doors and windows in good shape?

4. Does the interior hardware of your cabinetry work well? Do the doors and drawers open and close smoothly?

5. Are surfaces easy to maintain?

6. Are your gas, electrical, and other fuel sources in good repair?

7. How much time do you spend taking care of your kitchen every day? Every week?

8. What is the one cleanup chore you would most like to eliminate?

9. How many different cleaning products and machines do you use regularly?

10. Where does the mess accumulate fastest in your kitchen? Is there one area you just can't keep up with?

Final Thoughts

Both of the remodeled kitchens in this chapter express the character of well-loved, well-lived-in homes and the lifestyles of their owners. Design successes such as these are always the result of painstaking scrutiny, analysis, and preparation.

When planning a new kitchen, you must close your eyes and dream. But the real creativity occurs with your eyes wide-open.

ABOVE AND OPPOSITE A serving counter, exquisite from every angle, opens this beautiful kitchen to the living areas.
Design: Brininstool + Lynch

Your dream kitchen may be an ideal, but realizing it is a problem-solving process — time-consuming, labor-intensive, and often emotionally demanding. It involves moving through the known, as well as the unknown, limitations of your project. The wonderful irony is that the friction between imagination and reality will often spark your most creative design solutions. Limitations of space, light, money, or other resources can force you beyond the ordinary and into invention and unimagined beauty.

Part of the beauty of a well-balanced kitchen design is a well-balanced budget. Your new kitchen will be a wonderful gift for you and your loved ones. The process of building it, however, can take a lot out of you. Remember that design, like life, is a balancing act. If you pace yourself and your dollars, you won't run out of either.

four

budgeting your resources

In every kitchen, even the most grand, there are always some smart budgeting ideas to borrow. Every experienced designer is constantly grappling with the sensitive issue of how to spend money wisely and well.

The two kitchens designed by Chicago architect Brad Lynch (shown left and on pages 50 and 51) illustrate how the same aesthetic principles can be adapted to suit different budgets, with no loss of power or beauty. Although neither kitchen was inexpensive, the kitchen on pages 50 and 51 cost substantially less per square foot to build than the kitchen shown on the left. And while these designs are contemporary, the concepts we will discuss may be applied to traditional kitchens as well.

Both designs share Lynch's basic philosophy of treating architectural space like sculpture — a work of art that can be contemplated from any angle. Also, there is no "hierarchy" of rooms. As Lynch puts it, "No room is subservient to any other. All of the rooms work together and flow into each other, one anticipating the next, sometimes with a sense of mystery." And yet each space is separately defined, allowing it to function comfortably on its own.

Both of these kitchens are drawn in simple, clean lines and share a subdued palette of materials and colors. Light and dark tonalities are artfully balanced, and solid forms are set against open, light-filled spaces in a strong gridlike pattern of complementary vertical and horizontal elements.

In each, the views from the kitchen sink are expansive and exhilarating. Both designs are uncluttered and focused on only the essentials of kitchen operations. Even the minimal hardware repeats the shared aesthetic.

What makes one kitchen so much less expensive? Lynch used less-expensive materials: maple alone instead of maple in combination with more expensive wood; strip-maple floors instead of stone slabs (additionally cost-effective because wood flooring does not require the same strong substructure as stone flooring); and 1" dark-blue ceramic tiles on the backsplash in lieu of stone. Also, he sculpted the space with drywall, the least expensive of building materials.

Lynch applied many of the same principles to create the kitchen in chapter one (page 17), which cost even less per

square foot than either of the two kitchens we've just discussed. It's truly amazing what can be accomplished with space and light and a deft touch!

I have always believed in taking a slow and measured approach to design. You can acquire furnishings and housewares one beautiful piece at a time over many years — like a fine art collection — choosing quality over quantity, and making decisions that will last. You can start, as my husband and I did, with a few bargains such as the Barcelona chairs we bought early in our marriage from friends who were remodeling. With design choices that fit together and are part of an overall plan, you can slowly, surely, and effectively achieve your dream. We still have, and love, those chairs!

Opting for quality sometimes means taking the time to save for something you really want, such as a fine antique table or a granite countertop for your kitchen island. But it can also mean carefully refinishing hand-me-down furniture, waiting for sales, or scouring the flea markets.

When looking for long-term economy, I also believe in buying pieces in a consistent palette and in standard sizes and shapes: 8' x 10' area rugs in lieu of wall-to-wall carpet, tables for six instead of a built-in banquette, and three-seat sofas rather than large custom sofas. Should you move, these pieces stand the best chance of working in your next home. And even if you don't move, you'll be able to use them in new ways as your life changes through the years. The beautiful hutch that you buy today as a china cabinet may one day become a baking station in your kitchen or an entertainment center in your family room.

LEFT Bailey Edward Design paints a pretty and affordable kitchen picture in coral and blue laminate, achieving a wonderful effect that would not be possible with granite or marble. Open shelves (another money-saving strategy) with pop-through lights, suspended dramatically over the fluid forms of the island, complete the playful and practical decor.
Design: Bailey Edward Design

LEFT Glazed cabinets, open shelving, and contrasting finishes add depth and dimension to this small and charming country kitchen.
Design: Lisa McCauley

BELOW There's a return these days to linoleum to provide beautiful yet affordable flooring. Here the linoleum is cut with a border to suggest an area rug.
Design: Nancy Mullan

Although it's relatively easy to create something impressive with the most expensive materials, the real trick is creating beauty with modest materials. This concept — which I learned as a young student on my first day in art school — applies to any art form. Think about the extraordinary aesthetic power of a beautiful ceramic vase, and remember that it's made of earth. Or examine the delicate textures and patterns of a finely crafted basket made of straw. The beauty that you see in the forms comes from the heart and soul of the artist.

Of course, fine materials can enhance a kitchen design with their own innate beauty. But beautiful design must always begin and end with fundamental design principles. For example, if the line, proportions, and color of a couch are right, the fact that it is upholstered in canvas rather than leather will not detract from its beauty. The same principle applies to the overall design of your kitchen. Besides, you can always upgrade later — although people who follow this strategy often are so pleased with their initial choice that the thought of an upgrade quickly vanishes!

If you have your heart set on a particular material, such as granite for your countertops, but find that it won't fit neatly within your budget, consider using only a small amount of it. Mixing a variety of different countertop materials gives you not only design flexibility but also the luxury of having different countertops for different functions.

In general, veneers are less expensive than solid materials, and these days even synthetic materials are being fabricated as veneers to provide cost-saving alternatives for home owners.

Choosing materials in standard sizes can also reduce costs. For example, 12" x 12" marble tile is far more affordable than a solid slab. On the other hand, tiny tile mosaics laid out on a sheet can be more expensive because of the labor involved in making them.

In a remodeling, generally the best strategy for saving money is to preserve the existing footprint—avoiding the expense of modifying walls, windows, and other architectural elements, or of relocating appliances or lighting (which could require moving fuel or electrical lines, or plumbing).

Of course, it's always important to get the most out of the space you have, and many of the ideas in chapter nine may help. Also, you may find that one small change in the architecture can work wonders, making your existing kitchen space seem like a brand-new room. Sculpting spaces with standard, affordable drywall can transform a predictable, boxlike space.

I've toured many kitchens in which a narrow bump-out of just a few extra feet made a world of difference.

In designer Betty Torrell's *Mondrian Kitchen*
(right), both function and style were vastly enhanced by means
of creative and shrewdly economical solutions that expanded
the kitchen without a single major architectural adjustment.
The new plan improved storage and cooking, created an interior herb garden, conditioned the air, enhanced the views, and
made a powerful design statement by capitalizing on the
strengths of the existing space — recycling its best features,
selecting affordable materials, and following the personal
artistic vision of its owner.

OPPOSITE In order to balance both
the budget and the aesthetics of this
kitchen, a classic European range is
combined with affordable, vintage
pieces of freestanding cabinetry; a
custom-built wooden island; and
two simple tables.
Design: Luna Design Group

LEFT An arch over the
door and a recessed niche for the
cabinetry transform the
architecture of this space.
Design: Joan DesCombes

Ideas to help you stay on budget:

- **Save money on cabinets.** Cabinets are generally the single most expensive element in any kitchen design. Fortunately, there are many ways to save money:

  - Refinishing or replacing cabinet doors can make a huge improvement at a fraction of the cost of new cabinets.

  - Noting that fine finishes cause cabinetry prices to soar, one shrewd home enthusiast I know recommends selecting less-expensive cabinets and then painting over the finish. (When it comes to appliances, he shops for last year's models and doesn't mind a few scratches or dents.)

  - Resist the temptation to fill all available wall space with cabinets. Buy only the cabinets you need. Don't build so many that you are forced to shop to fill them when the kitchen is complete. The corollary is to streamline your kitchen supplies and equipment. I like the "one-of-each" rule: If you find one bowl that can be used for prep, storage, and serving, buy just that one. The less stuff you have, the fewer cabinets you need.

  - In lieu of a wall of costly cabinetry, use the space for something other than storage. Create a seating area, office space, or a place for the kids to play.

  - Flush-overlay cabinet doors generally are less costly than inset doors. Open shelves are decorative, provide easy access, and also save money.

- **Add life.** Real life makes any kitchen more beautiful, often at little or no extra cost. Plants and fresh flowers enrich any kitchen design. Books are also wonderful signs of life, with their vivid implications about the people who enjoy them. Add color and texture to your kitchen by making foods a living part of your decor. A bowl of fruit or a garland of dried chilies enliven a space for next to nothing.

- **Do it yourself.** Lots of money can be saved by doing some of the work, such as demolition or painting, yourself.

- **Avoid construction changes.** Nothing can drive up the cost of a new kitchen like making last-minute changes in the design plans. They can really throw a "money wrench" into the best-laid blueprints!

- **Shop at home . . . literally.** Bring in accessories and furniture from other rooms or the attic. And shop less by eliminating items you really don't need, such as window treatments (your kitchen can actually be enhanced by the extra light).

- **Create a single focal point.** Focus your investment where it will have the biggest impact. Then balance your design and your budget with more modest selections. A professional-style cooktop can add functional power and great presence to a kitchen, carrying the "weight" of the entire design. Make your design statement once, with one truly beautiful focal point; then allow the rest of the design to do its work with modest simplicity. Once you satisfy the eye's need for beauty, your mission is accomplished and you can let the other elements recede and take a secondary position. All it takes is a few special tiles on a field of standard tile to make your own personal statement on a backsplash. Use unadorned field tiles in your favorite color. A painted wall also works, and is the least-costly option.

- **Use salvaged or found materials.** The kitchen on page 60 is a wonderful example of how effective this idea can be. In an old farmhouse, the designer found a hutch that had lost its doors and was a mess. She painted it dark brown, then painted it white, and rubbed it down before applying a decorative motif inspired by tile in the room. Finally, she painted the inside blue and left it without doors. As a result, what might have been a discarded relic has become a richly decorative addition to a beautiful kitchen.

- **Invest in permanence.** The money you spend on architecture — space and light — is a lasting choice. You can always upgrade to finer appliances and materials later.

➤ **Avoid current trends.** For example, if you are flexible enough not to go with the current color trends, you can pick up a fine stone countertop at a more affordable price. One contractor I know suggests asking merchants what they "want to get rid of."

➤ **Choose a style that suits your pocketbook.** Some styles themselves suggest ways to economize. A minimalist approach can save you spare change if you really keep it minimal. The shabby chic approach gives you the chance to make the most of salvaged finds and flea-market treasures.

➤ **Make choices that perform a double function.** Plants can serve as a window screen and can also bring their own beauty and vitality to your kitchen. A decorative chest can hide the kids' toys and also serve as a window seat.

➤ **Monitor your momentum.** As the design process starts moving forward, it's easy to get carried away. The most dangerous words for a design budget can be "While we're at it . . ." If you go too far you can end up with excess space that you don't use, or rows of cabinets you don't need.

➤ **Kitchen design is not a race.** There is no finish line. Savor the pleasure of letting your kitchen design evolve and grow with you. Design is a lifelong process. Let your kitchen build slowly, one idea at a time.

➤ **Paint a new kitchen picture.** The most economical way to remodel your kitchen is with a fresh paint job. Whether you go wild with color or simply choose a coat of fresh white paint to revive old cabinet doors, you're literally applying a brand-new feeling to your kitchen.

OPPOSITE The home owner's idea of using a marigold yellow for the walls of this kitchen was initially a bit startling to the designer, who now loves the warmth and beauty that the color brings to the completed design.
Design: Rebecca Reynolds

ABOVE Found in an old farmhouse, this hutch had lost its doors and was a mess. Hand-painting has transformed a discarded relic into a richly decorative addition to a beautiful kitchen.
Design: Nancy Mullan

Painting one wall, an alcove, or the interiors of your cabinets with a strong shot of color can provide just the boost your kitchen needs. Pantries, mudrooms, and other small spaces adjoining your kitchen are also good candidates for new colors. Even appliances can be painted!

Professionals always say that meticulous preparation is the key to success when painting. It's true in kitchen design as well: Cleaning out cabinets, scraping away grime, and getting rid of the mismatched plastic wares hidden in the back corners of the cupboards will make any kitchen feel new.

So if a complete remodeling isn't in the cards right now, consider a new coat of paint to freshen up your kitchen while you're waiting.

Final Thoughts

Spending less money on your kitchen does not mean spending less creativity or enthusiasm. In fact, choosing to solve a design issue with an affordable solution often stimulates extraordinary thinking and leads you to a brand-new vision.

Whether you're designing on a shoestring or with an unlimited budget, your kitchen will be successful if it is a true expression of your values, tastes, and lifestyle. What I remember most after visiting someone's new kitchen is not the name of the material of the countertop or the particular details in the crown moldings. It's the people I met, and most of all their joyful enthusiasm as they shared their stories.

All kitchens include some ideas that are old, some that are new, some that are borrowed . . . but each must be you.

One of the greatest pleasures of design
is the joy of collecting ideas.

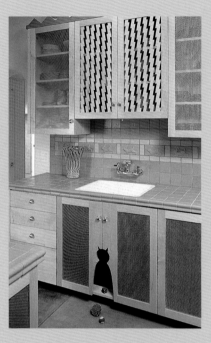

ABOVE This pueblo deco design takes its ideas from the desert sky and cactus flowers and from a special family member as well.

RIGHT The brightly colored floor, ceiling, and hand-painted tiles in the cooking arch bring an extraordinary vitality to this kitchen on the banks of the Rio Grande. And as if the color were not enough, the energy of this vision is reinforced by lightning-bolt cabinetry.
Design: Kathy Jackson

because of its life-enhancing power, design can be habit-forming. Design engages the imagination, bringing new insights and leading us to places we've never been. Making design an integral part of our daily lives teaches us to better see, feel, touch, smell, and taste the world in which we live. Best of all, design is active — it's something we *do!*

Inspiration and ideas are everywhere: in movies, in books and magazines, on TV, in the color of your eyes, and in the pattern on those socks you bought your father for his birthday. The hot color for today's cars may well end up on tomorrow's refrigerator. The fabrics on your new kitchen chairs may be a by-product of space technology.

five

collecting ideas

Ideas Come from Your Lifestyle

Designers know the importance of listening carefully to their clients. One designer I know gives all new clients an exhaustive, eighteen-page questionnaire to fill out in preparation for their first design consultation. Specific details, even down to your recycling habits, where the dog sleeps in the afternoon, and your annual lobster fest, will help you plan a kitchen that serves your specific needs. The questionnaire in chapter three can really help you to "get specific." It may also jog your memory about things you simply take for granted.

Ideas Come from Kitchens You Visit

Here are a dozen ideas suggested by this lovely kitchen, built in a large home on the shores of Lake Michigan. See if you can find more!

➢ Accent your center island with "end tables" that match the cabinetry in the rest of your kitchen.

➢ Use straight-backed chairs in lieu of stools at a breakfast bar.

➢ Continue the kitchen flooring into the adjacent breakfast room.

➢ Divide space using a glass-paneled portal.

- Warm, knotty pine cabinetry softens even a grand design such as this.
- Roman shades suspended from a curtain rod make a handsome valance when open.
- Plates make beautiful decorative accents throughout a kitchen space.
- A pot-filler faucet over the range avoids the drudgery of carrying heavy pots from the sink.
- Integrated granite sinks provide handsome continuity in a kitchen design.
- A niche behind the hearth is the perfect place for everyday cooking necessities, such as olive oil and salt and pepper.
- Mixing countertop materials adds variety, depth, and utility to a kitchen design.
- A finely detailed ceiling can have a powerful impact.

OPPOSITE AND ABOVE
Every idea you borrow will be transformed by the way you adapt it to your own kitchen.
Design: Scott Himmel and Mick De Giulio

ABOVE Even if contemporary
styling doesn't suit you, the idea
of building "two steps up" may be
the perfect way to separate your
family room from your kitchen
while retaining an open plan.
Design: Dianne Harsch

Ideas Come from Pictures

Magazines, of course, are the place to start. Here are some
techniques to help you become a really good design detective:

> Don't limit yourself. Give every image a chance, whether
> it's a kitchen or not. You may find the perfect kitchen
> window treatment in a library or a living room, in a base-
> ment or an attic.

➤ Save every photograph that you fall in love with, whether it seems relevant or not. Do you find yourself looking at images of nature or are you more attracted to urban scenes? Do you gravitate toward photos filled with people or do you prefer pictures with few, if any, people in them?

➤ You may not understand why something appeals to you now, but as your collection of images increases, understandable patterns will emerge. You may discover things about your taste that you couldn't have predicted. Designers have told me that clients with stacks of photos are often surprised when, after some discussion, they realize that all of the pictures reflect the same design theme (almost as if they were different shots of the same kitchen).

➤ Just as important as knowing what you like is knowing what you *don't* like. So collect those pictures too! This can provide you and your design team with an invaluable shortcut to understanding your taste.

➤ Don't give up on a photograph until you've really looked at it carefully. You may not like the brash colors you see, but the clerestory windows may be just the architectural adjustment your kitchen needs. The flowery wallpaper may overwhelm the photo, but the design of the center island might be just what you've been looking for!

➤ Train your eye. Challenge yourself to find at least one good idea in every bad picture. Then try the opposite: It's even more challenging to find design flaws in pictures you love!

RIGHT This kitchen may convince you that having a limited kitchen footprint does not mean having a limited kitchen vision.
Design: Barbara Houston

The wallpaper border on the pantry backsplash — with its abundant array of vegetables over a classic frieze that is ornamented with animal faces — inspired the mood, colors, and textures for an entire kitchen.
Design: Chip Webster

Ideas Come from Objects

Kitchen designs can be inspired by a teapot collection, a vintage stove, your grandmother's apron, an antique sampler, an Andy Warhol poster, or just about anything else you love!

LEFT All the ideas in this kitchen were inspired by the home owner's favorite shade of green and the rich colors and bucolic warmth of a beloved collection of Quimper pottery from France.
Design: Mick De Giulio

OPPOSITE This kitchen floor borrows its geometric pattern from the dining-room rug next door.
Design: Erica Broberg

RIGHT AND BELOW The design cues for this backsplash were taken from the upholstery, wallpaper, and vivacious personality of the home owner, who, according to the artist, "needed the fiery red."
Tile design: Lisa Breznak

LEFT AND BELOW To redefine the kitchen entry, two charming, eye-catching columns were built above half walls. With proportions that take a sharp turn away from traditional models, they appear disarmingly appropriate. When asked how he came up with their unique design, the architect explained that they were copies of original columns on the opposite side of this kitchen.

Similarly, the design for the cabinet doors was picked up from the windows on the facade of the home. Glazing was continued onto the back door to take advantage of the view of the patio.

Design: Andre Rothblatt

Ideas Come from Architecture

For continuity, consider following the patterns set by your home's exterior and interior architecture.

ABOVE A semicircular wall of windows and an arched window above suggested the curvilinear lines of cabinetry, as well as the form of the center island.
Design: Siemasko + Verbridge

RIGHT The rope molding over the hearth of this Old English design was copied from an archway over the front door of the house, imparting a subtle architectural harmony to the overall design.
Design: Stephen A. Kinon and Fran Murphy

LEFT In order to build a sink under the original seed-glass window in a style that would match the flair of the rest of the kitchen design, an inventive designer and "tinkering-type" home owner changed the double-hung window into a barn sash that opens into the kitchen and is suspended from the ceiling by a chain.
Design: Beth Veillette

BELOW Because they couldn't move it, they used it! A structural column becomes part of an abstract composition of contrasting curved and angular forms made of concrete, exotic wood, and natural stone that brings interest to this contemporary kitchen island.
Design: Gioi Tran and Vernon Applegate

Ideas Come from Solving Problems

The Old English kitchen on the opposite page is a wonderful illustration of how a design problem ultimately led to an inventive solution. The problem: How do you design an island with a dishwasher and still maintain a classic English feel? The solution: Panel the dishwasher and surround it with a custom cabinet with turned legs and a shelf. The legs give the piece the look of furniture while decorative accessories draw attention away from the solid mass of the dishwasher itself.

RIGHT Exotic foreign adventures are remembered every day in this Asian-influenced design, featuring carved elephants and plant forms, a bamboo ceiling fan, and a dark-brown mahogany island with polished brass hardware and stepped detailing at the base. At the hearth, under an antique carving from Thailand, a fabric mural is protected by a glass frame.
Design: Christine Julian

BELOW As revealed by this detail, the inspiration for these kitchen cabinets came from the home owner's love of the paintings of Dutch artist Piet Mondrian. The kitchen is featured in chapter twelve.
Design: Betty Torrell

Ideas Come from Exploring the World

The romance of travel inspires people to bring home design ideas from new places. Southwestern, Tuscan, Asian, African, and Moroccan styles are just a few of the popular motifs.

Museums are massive collections of great

ideas. Whatever draws your curiosity may be just what your kitchen needs.

This kitchen owes much of its serene beauty to its unobstructed views of lush gardens and a spectacular lake. Its soothing tones of gentle green were taken directly from the jade color of the water just beyond the kitchen windows.
Design: Joan DesCombes

Ideas Come from Exploring Your Neighborhood

Your neighborhood may be your starting point. What are its special charms? Is there a mood that drew you there that you'd like to repeat in your kitchen? Is there a little café you love, with a decor that pleases you?

Ideas Come from Collaboration

Some of the best design ideas emerge from the synergy created by a team of creative people, each member bringing his or her own individual strengths to the process.

The design on the left began with a unique oval window, an old pine hutch, and an enthusiastic belief that it's possible to find a place for everything you love! The apparent spontaneity of this casual family kitchen is actually the result of lots of serious teamwork. It took the combined talents of a kitchen designer, an architectural team, and the home owner / interior designer to find graceful solutions to the many design issues of the project, including how to make the oval window fit into both the kitchen and dining room, how to design new cabinetry to complement the older pieces, and how to make it all fit in a somewhat awkward raw space.

ABOVE The easy charm of this kitchen design took months of serious planning.
Design: Stuart Cohen & Julie Hacker Architects; Christine Julian; and Stephanie Wohlner

RIGHT Inspired by the efficiency and orderliness of her computer's desktop, the owner of this London Minimal kitchen wanted an uncluttered space that would hide maximum function behind smooth and simple surfaces.
Design: Mick De Giulio

Ideas Come from Your Personal Philosophy, Your Goals, and Your Spirit

You may be surprised at how your outlook on life can impact your design — whether you're selecting colors, drawing a floor plan, or making a thematic statement.

Final Thoughts

Sourcing ideas for your new kitchen is like going on a treasure hunt — with the whole world to poke through. But, fair warning: It's definitely addictive. I have a friend who spent every Saturday for an entire year at the Chicago Public Library reading European design magazines and books until she found the precise focus for her new kitchen design — and she says she'd do it again!

ABOVE This tile backsplash, inspired by a vacation snapshot of a mosaic floor in an ancient church, signals a deeply personal belief about the importance of opening your home and sharing its bountiful gifts.
Design: Jean Stoffer

LEFT The idea for this kitchen floor came from breakfast!
Design: Stephen and Wendy Gardner

It's not just in your head! Taste is a total mind-body phenomenon, requiring input from all of your senses.

ABOVE AND OPPOSITE Your comfort is the key to making choices that fit.
Design: Nancy Mullan [above], Brininstool + Lynch [opposite]

Our bodies know the rough texture of a rush seat, the quick glide across smooth leather, the soft give of down cushions. We remember the sensations of cool glass, warm wood, soft limestone, hard steel. It's no wonder that so many of our best design choices are based on gut instinct. And what better way to choose a style for your new kitchen than to imagine yourself at the kitchen table, where so many of us begin and end each day.

So in this chapter we have deliberately narrowed our focus and aimed the camera at seating areas. These photos are intended to draw you in to a variety of beautiful styles, allowing you to *feel* them from the inside out.

Let's take a *Goldilocks and the Three Bears* kitchen-design tour. Try each chair for size . . . and see which one is just right for you!

six

choosing your style

ABOVE LEFT Gentle colors and textures combine to create an approachable formality in this "farmhouse romantic" kitchen. Note the blue-and-white embroidered linen tablecloth, layered over a midnight-blue undercloth edged with a delicate, geometric pattern. The design on the linens is echoed in the china, the armoire, and the hand-decorated chairs. With roses on the table, this room exudes an inviting fragrance.
Design: Nancy Mullan

ABOVE RIGHT All is space, light, and form in this serene, uncomplicated space. With a view into the garden (landscaped with native plantings in keeping with the understated nature of the design) and a view through the woods toward a lake, the seating area features millwork components, light fixtures, and a dining table that were custom designed using steel frames, clear-coated wood, and glass.
Design: Brininstool + Lynch

ABOVE LEFT This seating area is a warm and friendly study in contrasts. The rich cherry-wood bay is decorated with a carved–coastal shell motif, an inlaid floor, and delicate, leaded-glass windows. The cathedral ceiling is constructed of knotty pine while pale, rough beams sit over an elegant, glazed china cabinet with a stepped-edge granite countertop.
Design: Thomas Richard Kelly

ABOVE RIGHT Talk about space and light! On a brick patio just outside the kitchen door sits this simple, all-season table and chairs. As if in response to the home owners' obvious reverence for nature, the aged trees graciously provide the walls and ceiling for this lovely dining area.
Design: Marmol Radziner + Associates

ABOVE LEFT There is an unmistakable sense of weightlessness in this artfully sculpted, contemporary breakfast booth. The tabletop, with an undercut edge and tapered supporting legs, floats above the cantilevered seats, coming to rest at the soft curve of the sill beneath the bay window. A single graceful flower in the integrated countertop vase repeats the sinuous cord of the suspended light fixture.
Design: Fu-Tung Cheng

ABOVE RIGHT Under a profusion of leaves, we are magically transported into a garden for breakfast. White-on-white textures of tiles, moldings, painted surfaces, and inset paneled doors are accented by a bouquet of yellow tulips and a few eggs. In their natural simplicity, these elements recall the Arts and Crafts movement.
Design: Stuart Cohen & Julie Hacker Architects

ABOVE LEFT This rich red banquette, set in a gently curving bay, provides a transition from the working kitchen (with its counter seating), through the family room, and to the outside. The round, woven floor mat completes the circle suggested by the arc of the bench, establishing the banquette as a separate zone — one of a series of interrelated areas for enjoying food and the view.
Design: Mary Douglas Drysdale

ABOVE RIGHT Fine materials are presented with refinement to create this warm and elegant kitchen banquette. The detailing of the deco-inspired table base and the dark chairs contrasts with the clean lines of the curved paneling (illuminated by cove lighting) and the upholstered bench below. A delicate task light floats over the table while shelves of candy add a sweet, friendly touch.
Design: Bruce Bierman Design, Inc.

LEFT This regal seating area, a cozy spot within a highly functional, professional-style kitchen, was inspired by the tradition of a restaurant chef's table.
Design: Pamela Bytner

RIGHT Soft upholstered cushions and pillows, two period chairs, shelves of vintage dishware, and a particularly charming array of 1930s Bakelite tools set the mood in this inviting banquette seating area.
Design: Jack Murchie and Marta Gazda Auskalnis

Final Thoughts

When it comes to designing your kitchen, all the art history classes in the world and consultations with the finest architects and designers won't mean a thing unless your body agrees with your mind. In order to be successful, your kitchen design must elicit a strong and positive visceral response in you. It must *feel right*.

LEFT At the apex of two fully equipped cooking stations, this sun-drenched breakfast room projects into the garden, collecting light and a beautiful view of the terrace. Mullioned windows reach up to the octagonal wood ceiling in this cozy conservatory.
Design: Adolfo Perez

ABOVE Coordinated window and wall fabrics join with a vibrantly colored landscape painting to enliven this classic breakfast area. An 1840s English gateleg table, bow-back chairs, and bead-board wainscoting complete this cozy corner.
Design: Sally Cernik Weston

Nobody cares more about your new kitchen than you, except for the most dedicated members of your design team.

ABOVE AND OPPOSITE
These old cabinets got a *brand*-new look with a branding iron, and the new hardware was given an aged patina.
Design: Clodagh

W hatever the scale of your project, kitchen design always involves teamwork. Choosing the right people to guide you will help you fulfill your creative vision and take much of the stress out of problem solving. After all, what may seem like an insurmountable hurdle to you might well be a commonplace reality to an architect, designer, or other expert. As the leader of your design team, you are the one who must carefully select the players.

Design help is widely available today. In addition to references from friends and family, you can rely on many manufacturers and retailers to offer assistance, and organizations such as the National Kitchen + Bath Association, the American Institute of Architects, and the American Society of Interior Designers can also help you put together the right design team.

seven

your design team

This morning I had a 10:00 A.M. phone appointment with New York designer Clodagh to discuss the details of a San Francisco kitchen she designed for Agnes Bourne and her husband, James Luebbers.

I was looking forward to our conversation. Interviewing people of such ability, even long-distance, is one of the most exhilarating aspects of my work. Suddenly, the kitchen pictures on my desk blossom before my eyes. Everything becomes vivid, I see more details, and I come to truly understand the design.

Because of its alluring appeal, "Stone House, SF" (the name on the label of the photographs on my desk) had captured my interest from the moment I first saw it. Then, after hearing the unbridled delight in Clodagh's voice as she described Agnes and Jim, their vision, and the design team that brought the kitchen to life, I realized that Clodagh had given me a real gift: the story of how joyful and enthusiastic a collaboration can be. The scope of this project may have been grand, but fundamentally it's a simple story about how an extraordinary team was assembled in order to express Agnes and Jim's passionate energy for life in an earthy, comfortable, and "gathering" kitchen.

So many design stories begin with a little click: that moment of clarity when both the designer and the client feel the rapport — the shared sympathy — that tells them they are a good match. This matching is usually about more than line, form, and color. It's about finding design partners with whom you share common values and from whom you can learn. The best matches are between people who are as eager to listen as they are to share their own views. There was definitely a click for Agnes, Jim, and Clodagh.

Clodagh spoke fondly of Agnes, a well-known designer of interiors and furniture, and her husband, a doctor and the cook in the family. Both Jim and Agnes wanted a high-performance kitchen that would be "all about eating." It also had to be large enough so that Jim could give cooking lessons — or bring in another chef to teach. Plus, the couple has three children and three grandchildren, so this had to be a room that would draw them all in and keep them together comfortably.

After talking to her clients about everything from how they entertain large groups to how Jim cooks and where he likes to store his measuring spoons, Clodagh now took the next step — examining the existing kitchen to see what it had to say. Architecture can be persuasive and demanding, and often the best ideas for a new vision come from walking through the space and listening to the walls. Together with Agnes and Jim, Clodagh and her architect partner, Robert Pierpont, began devining, editing, cleansing, demolishing, sorting, and imagining what-if.

Originally for servants, this kitchen was built downstairs, partly below grade, in a stately 1894 neoclassic house with a view of the bay. Knowing that Agnes loves crisp color and that San Francisco can be gray and misty, Clodagh filled the room with its own sunshine. Polished integrated-color plaster walls (sealed, because Clodagh doesn't believe in maintenance!) create an apricot-and-ochre glow that spills out into the adjoining hallway. There is a living pulse emanating from these walls, partly from the ripe reddish highlights and partly from the energy that was imbedded in them by this design team.

After a raucous but friendly competition to come up with their favorite quotations, Jim, Agnes, and Clodagh were joined by artisans from a company called Art in Construction, and together they sponged, scratched, and stenciled the wisdom of Winnie the Pooh, the voices of Anaïs Nin and Edith Wharton (and others), along with their own thoughts on a frieze supported by highly theatrical, 12' high "leaning" columns. A massive stainless hood hovers over a no-nonsense work island, and the original cabinetry was restored and then "branded" with branding irons made by artist Alan Swanson (another member of the team) to add yet one more rich layer to the room's patina. The original doors were saved but refined with new metal framing, up lights, and art-glass transoms (created by team members John Degnan and Duncan Laurie) to emphasize their verticality.

Because the room is spacious, Swanson had space enough to build a large rectory table (designed by Clodagh) that seats twelve and is also sealed for easy care. In the corner beyond the table, high enough so that guests can see into the cooking area, are two "squishy" down-filled lounges upholstered in tough and durable silks of ochre, with written graphics in gold and with apricot, burgundy, and gray accent pillows. The tower of three TV monitors that looks like art was planned so that Jim could watch a cooking program while Agnes and the grandchildren listened on headphones to their own favorite shows.

The clever little reading light near the window was made from old car parts by artist Daniel Berglund. Feng shui expert Sarah Rossback also collaborated on the project, suggesting ideas to heighten the emotional richness of the kitchen. A mirrored backsplash behind the sink reflects the light and amplifies the abundance of foodstuffs displayed (by Steven Watkins) on the concrete-and-steel inset counter. Up lights are balanced against down lights. The soft sound of splashing water from the small fountain, along with the smell of Jim's cooking, make this a design for all the senses.

Clodagh talks about designing "experiences" rather than rooms. This kitchen is an obvious success on that score. But what impressed me most was the lilt in her voice as she spoke of the delight shared by everyone who worked together on this kitchen. This was clearly a labor of love, and clearly focused on bringing joy to Agnes and Jim.

There is often a family feeling that develops when a small group of dedicated people join forces to meet a common goal. What an inspiration!

On Choosing and Working with Your Design Team:

➤ Ask friends to recommend designers, workpeople, architects, and engineers they trust. Or seek help at your local home-improvement center or favorite retail store. Many of these companies offer design advice free of charge.

➤ Choose team members who are as highly trained as possible. You can avoid costly mistakes by working with skilled professionals. Getting things right the first time saves money.

➤ When interviewing prospective team members, ask for specific examples of how they've solved problems on other projects. If they don't have an answer, interview more candidates.

➤ Ask pointed questions about their training and experience. What was their favorite job? What was their least-favorite job? Always request multiple references.

➤ A good designer challenges clients to stretch their design tastes, but good clients challenge designers as well.

➤ There must be a feeling of connection between a designer and a client, and the listening must go both ways.

➤ Ask your team members whom they like to work with. There's nothing better than a track record of trust and respect.

➤ Make all of your decisions in a dialogue with your design team. Luckily, you're not alone!

➤ Design is an organic, dynamic process; be flexible and spontaneous and let the process "breathe." Calculate your risks and don't be paralyzed by a fear of the unknown. Before you reject a new idea, revisit it at least once or twice.

➤ Teamwork demands sensitivity. From time to time a "beautiful tension" between clients and designers may arise. Recognize this as an inevitable part of the problem-solving process. It is often wise to allow designers, craftspeople, and artists the freedom that they require to do their best work. You also have to know, however, when to take the lead. Great designs emerge from what one designer called "that wonderful chaotic mess" — always a result of give-and-take.

On Surviving Construction:

➤ Don't be afraid of construction problems. Many designers and clients have stories about how a mistake or problem turned into an advantage because it forced them to put their heads together to find a solution. Often this solution turns out to be something new and wonderful that neither expected. And what impresses me most is that frequently they don't remember "who thought of what" — a very good indication of how closely they were working!

➤ Be diligent about visiting the construction site. A daily check is not too often. Remember, little changes at the right time are affordable and can be very wise. Also, spotting a major mistake early on will save everybody a lot of aggravation later.

➤ Beware of making major changes once you're under way. They can cause serious budgetary overruns. Take all the time you need in advance to be certain that you know what you want.

➤ Keep a notebook with the first and last names and all the phone and pager numbers of the people with whom you are working. Invest the time necessary to develop a good system of communication. Checking in regularly by telephone or e-mail can be very effective.

➤ Keep a log of your conversations with your design and construction teammates and others. This may help eliminate unnecessary confusion later.

➤ Before construction, prepare a dedicated entry into your home for the construction crew.

- Try not to let the demolition work begin until all your new cabinets and appliances are ready to be delivered.

- Have weekly face-to-face meetings with the key members of your design and construction teams to discuss goals, budgeting concerns, and scheduling issues, and to facilitate decision making.

- Don't rush to install the cabinets. If they are installed too soon (for example, before floors are finished), they may be damaged. And while the cabinets are being stored, be sure they are in an environment with temperature and humidity similar to your kitchen. Storing them in a garage, especially in humid regions, can damage them. (It's also advisable to have hardwood flooring delivered in plenty of time to let it expand or contract in its new environment prior to installation.)

- Allow ample time to clear out your kitchen prior to construction. Don't do it the night before your builder is scheduled to arrive. Pack everything in boxes two to eight weeks ahead of time. This is a good opportunity to take stock of your kitchen equipment and to group items together for your new space.

- Remove pictures and other items from the walls in rooms adjacent to your work site so that they don't get knocked off the wall or otherwise damaged during construction.

- Seal off your construction area with at least two layers of plastic sheeting. Choose a contractor to be responsible for this job, or take the time necessary to do it yourself. Place damp towels at the bottom of the sheeting to control dust.

- Don't move out of your house. If you're not there, no one is. (I've heard the opposite too; a designer I know said you should go to a hotel — or a friend's house — for a month or two!)

- Set up a sensible temporary kitchen in another room. You can move the essentials — the refrigerator, toaster, coffeemaker, hot plate, and microwave — to a convenient location such as a garage or laundry room (preferably a room with a sink).

- Confirm in advance that your contractor will be responsible for site cleanup and safety every day.

- Strive to keep your daily routines as balanced as possible. While you may be willing to temporarily forgo some of your usual activities in order to find the time to handle your kitchen project, it's always a good idea to keep these little sacrifices to a minimum.

- Be mentally prepared for delays. Anticipate frustration and chaos. Embrace it as part of the process.

- Be realistic. In every remodeling job you will inevitably reach the point of no return, when you've "just had it." When that happens, you should spend a weekend away. Figure it into your budget. The designer who suggested this is now planning to give each new client a gift certificate for one night in a hotel!

- Take-out menus are invaluable, so keep a good supply within easy reach of the phone!

- Don't plan a wedding or any other special occasion for the day after your anticipated date of completion.

ALL IMAGES
Design: Clodagh

Joan's Five Rules of Thumb

Here are five fundamentals to keep in mind from start to finish, to help you avoid many common mistakes and discover some exciting solutions.

❶ Assume Nothing

Making assumptions is like taking a shortcut for the first time through dense woods — it's tempting, but you run the risk of getting lost.

➢ Just because your friend is thrilled with the work of her design consultant or interior decorator, do not assume that you will work well with that same person. Think long and hard before you choose anyone for your design team or building crew. Is this individual's personality compatible with yours? Will this person understand your point of view and respect your needs and opinions? Do you like the work that he or she has done for other clients? And always get multiple references!

➢ You may be convinced that a kitchen island is the most practical design concept since the invention of the wheel. But do not automatically assume that an island is the best, or only, answer for your space. Explore all the options. Talk to your designer or other happy kitchen owners. You may end up with a completely different solution, reviving an idea that's been over-looked for years, or inventing a new design concept all your own.

❷ Never Take No for an Answer (at Least, Not Right Away)

When someone says "It can't be done," remember that some design problems have unexpected solutions. Before you accept no for an answer, take some extra time to think things through; there may be a yes out there. Talk to others, or try to come up with a solution of your own. Precisely because you are not a professional, you may find the unconventional solution to the problem you need to solve.

No one cares more about your home than you. So when your designer or contractor says it can't be done, don't accept that answer right away. Bring your own focused intelligence and creativity to bear on the problem. You'll be amazed at what you come up with!

❸ Never Take Yes for an Answer Either

Even small-scale projects can become extremely complex, pulling your attention in several different directions at once. When this happens, it's tempting to take yes for an answer without making absolutely sure that your instructions and wishes are clearly understood. It is easy to accept assurances that everything is going along according to your specifications and schedule — without checking for yourself. But be watchful! Reviewing the work in progress, asking questions, and clarifying instructions will save you time, money, and regret.

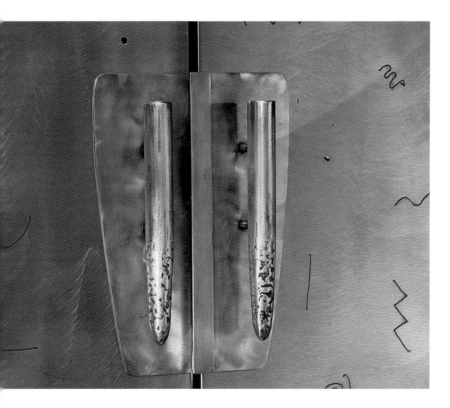

❹ Be Unsophisticated

There is no such thing as a dumb question when it comes to getting the new kitchen you want. Don't have false expectations of yourself. Your expertise will grow over time. Never be embarrassed to ask (or reiterate) questions that will allow you to thoroughly understand whatever you need to know. This is especially true when dealing with buzzwords. If an interior designer or contractor uses words that you don't understand, stop the conversation and ask for an explanation. Avoid the temptation to nod your head and smile knowingly when you really don't understand something. You owe it to yourself and your pocketbook to be unsophisticated.

❺ Think Backward

It's easy to look ahead when you start a kitchen-design project, imagining that glorious day when you will walk into your wonderful new kitchen and fix breakfast in style and comfort. This kind of forward thinking is essential to the exciting planning phase. But when it comes to the rough-and-tumble construction phase, you'll be in much better shape if you also remembered to think backward in the planning stage.

Once you have envisioned your final design goal, identify all the myriad tasks that need to be accomplished in order to achieve that goal. Getting your dream kitchen, or just a new sconce on the wall, requires planning, sourcing, ordering, delivery, and installation. Depending on your situation, it may also include demolition or removal of existing features, as well as repairs such as patching, painting, or repapering walls.

Your architect and contractor can do most of this, but they may also forget things. You'll need to research, make phone calls, and do some serious legwork yourself. Thinking backward and identifying all the steps involved in your project *before* you get started will give you a big boost in getting the job done on time, on budget, and to your satisfaction.

Final Thoughts

Be patient, keep your sense of humor, and remember, it will be worth it in the end. Most important of all, remember that, in the realm of all possible problems, design problems are good problems to have.

part two:

the five building blocks of kitchen design

In today's kitchen, beauty and function are inseparable.

O f the five building blocks of kitchen design, function comes first. Every decision you make about how you want your kitchen to work affects the aesthetics of your design, and every decision you make about aesthetics affects important functional issues as well.

The first and most fundamental question is "What's it for?" How do you want to live and work in your new kitchen? Is this a room for cooking or just for warming and serving, where all you need is a telephone and a few take-out menus? Is this a kitchen for Thanksgiving dinner or just for snacks? Is it "only for show" or a vital arena in which to conduct all the complex business of daily life? The way you want to use your new kitchen will inspire, and may even dictate, many of your design choices.

ABOVE A rugged hearth adds handsome styling, a baking oven, and an open grill.
Design: Chip Webster

OPPOSITE This high-tech, function-first "kitchen machine" even has drains in the floor so it can be hosed down at the end of a party!
Design: Joan DesCombes

eight

function

BELOW AND RIGHT Freestanding hutches are a wonderful alternative to standard shelves and cupboards. These mission-inspired pieces are packed with contemporary function: a gift-wrapping station, complete with a drop-down surface for quick projects and a chalkboard for memos, and a charming play station sporting a fanciful column that makes it easy to find just the right crayon.
Design: Lisa McCauley

It's best to begin by considering broad functional issues such as these:

➢ **How important is cooking?** Are you a gourmet chef, or would you be just as happy if you could turn your range into a planter and use your dishwasher as a file cabinet? (Don't laugh; I know someone who did just that!)

➢ **Do you like to entertain lavishly,** in small groups, or not at all? Are holiday dinners always at your home, or do you wish they were? If you entertain a lot, do you use caterers?

➢ **Do you want to eat in your kitchen?** If so, how much seating do you need, and what kind of seating should it be? Should you have a large or small table, a counter with stools, a nook, a banquette, or perhaps a cozy lounge chair or two?

➢ **Do you have a large family or do you live alone?** Is your family growing or are you an empty nester?

➢ **Does your family include pets** whose needs must be accommodated in the design?

ABOVE Set apart in an arched recess, this kitchen desk creates a perfect place for quiet work.
Design: Mary Douglas Drysdale

ABOVE RIGHT Business becomes pleasure when a custom hutch discreetly holds the family computer, file storage, bookcase, and decorative built-in clock. Traditionally styled and finely detailed with inlays and leaded glass, its function is strictly modern.
Design: Lisa McCauley

➢ **How much storage do you require?** Do you need a large butler's pantry for storing silver and glassware, or just a small cabinet for a few canned goods?

➢ **Do you dream of your new kitchen** as a busy gathering place for friends and family, or a quiet place for a cup of tea and a good book? Does either dream include a fireplace?

➢ **Is ease of maintenance** a high priority?

➢ **Do you want a wet bar** in your kitchen?

➢ **Will your kitchen serve as an office** for household management or a home-based business, or as a message center with space for a calendar, phone, and computer?

➢ **Do you envision using your kitchen for hobbies?** Do you want a place for your wine collection or a potting sink? Would you like your children to do their homework or arts and crafts projects in the kitchen?

> **How should your kitchen relate functionally** to your other rooms? Should it open onto, or be part of, a family room, dining room, mudroom, or laundry room? I know of one kitchen in a large, turn-of-the-century Boston home where a mother of three young boys included not only a washer and dryer but also her kids' closets and bathroom. Coming in from playing, the boys dump their dirty clothes right in the hamper, bathe, and put on clean clothes without tramping mud through the house!

> **How do you want your kitchen** to relate to the outdoors? Should it open onto a patio, or should part of the cooking function, such as a grill, be outside? Is there a particularly beautiful view that can be captured through thoughtfully placed windows?

> **Do you require,** or anticipate the need for, wheelchair accessibility or accommodations for other special needs for you or members of your family?

ABOVE In this kitchen, one dry sink and one wet sink were brought together to make watering plants and arranging flowers an effortless kitchen pleasure.
Design: Cynthia S. Muni and Sandra R. Williams

Once you have decided on the general functional requirements of your new kitchen, you can focus on more specific issues:

> **Precisely how do you cook?** Do you favor high-tech gear or conventional appliances? These days, we are no longer restricted to the simple choice of gas versus electric cooking. Modern ranges have evolved to include both in one, as well as other new technologies. Are you interested in some of the modern, health-conscious, water-based cooking appliances such as steam ovens or sinks with integrated steam-cooking units? Modular elements are also a valuable option, enabling you to mix and match traditional ranges with deep fryers and grills, or even a wok burner, pizza oven, or wood-burning rotisserie. If you're working with limited space, you might investigate the newest miniaturized cooking appliances that not only take up less room but also serve multiple functions such as microwaving, grilling, broiling, and baking.

> **Is there more than one cook in your family?** If so, you may want to create multiple workstations.

> **If you use caterers,** would it be useful to have a separate prep area or secondary kitchen for them to work in?

> **Do you want to maximize counter space?** Under-the-counter microwave ovens and refrigerators are options worth considering. Plus, they are handy for kids!

> **Do you like to bake?** You might plan for a dedicated baking area, with a stone countertop for kneading dough and rolling out piecrusts. Consider building it lower than your other countertops for comfort and accessibility.

> **Do you cook on the run?** Perhaps a warming drawer for carryout food is just the thing for you. Warming drawers are also great for home owners who entertain a lot.

> **Is speed of preparation important?** There are appliances geared to that as well, such as ovens that combine microwave and convection technologies to dramatically decrease cooking time, and new electronic cooktops that heat up virtually as quickly as gas burners.

> **Is easy maintenance a high priority?** If so, you may wish to trade in your high-tech, high-BTU gas range for a sleek, easy-to-clean electric model with a smooth glass surface that wipes up instantly.

> **Do you want a full entertainment center** in your kitchen to draw others in, or just a radio or small TV for your personal use while you cook or grab breakfast before work?

ABOVE This indoor basketball court, within easy shouting distance of the kitchen sink, keeps the whole family together — an idea inspired by thinking in new and unexpected ways. To call it a playful kitchen might be the understatement of the year. **Design: Stuart Cohen & Julie Hacker Architects and Jennifer Morgenstern**

In a compact city apartment, big ideas sometimes have to take up less space. But as designer Yves-Claude proves, a lot of function can be packed into a small kitchen footprint without any loss of style.

In any kitchen built for real cooking, appliances are the most powerful pieces of the puzzle. They literally take up the most space, and they set the standard both functionally and aesthetically for every other design decision. Often a shopping trip to the appliance mart is the first step home owners take as they begin to plan. And in this small urban kitchen, where the goal was to achieve the highest level of cooking function, handsome professional-grade appliances were the inevitable point of departure. Unlike many kitchens in which the appliances are visually integrated with the cabinetry, in this room all the cabinetry is custom-built to match the appliances.

Satin-finish stainless steel was chosen not just "to match" and not just for its innate reflective beauty, but also for the durability, heat resistance, and safety it offers as an extremely hygienic surface. Function is enhanced by a vertical pullout pantry (its handle "borrowed" from the refrigerator), a chop-

ping block hidden in a drawer, gull-wing doors that flip overhead, and a blind corner unit that pulls everything out and forward. Handy towel bars (at tummy level) have the extra benefit of shielding cooks and their aprons from messy, wet countertops.

Another benefit is the removable kick plates that reveal the 4" legs upon which all the cabinets are built, making maintenance and cleanliness a breeze.

Walls and a floor of rich green marble surround this compact assemblage of modular (and readily portable) furniture pieces to complete the transformation of a standard apartment kitchen into a sturdy and sophisticated twenty-first-century space.

ABOVE AND OPPOSITE
Because if its neutrality, stainless steel is equally at home in both contemporary and traditional kitchens.
Design: Yves-Claude

For many families, the call from inside the kitchen is no longer that decades-old warning "Go away and close the door. I'll call you when dinner's ready!" Instead, it's "C'mon in, the more the merrier!" The kitchen door, if there is one, is wide-open. That's certainly the case with this kitchen, in a project the designer, Joan DesCombes, calls *Together in the Kitchen.*

In order to meet the needs of five (and soon to be six) children, Mom, Dr. Dad, and a cook/housekeeper, three unappealing rooms with various ceiling and floor heights and numerous doors, walls, and windows ("all in the wrong places") were converted into one multifunctional space that controls and coordinates traffic in this house better than a full-time crossing guard!

The space is composed of five separate areas, each with a distinct function. Directly across from the hearth, the main island (with prep sink and refrigerator) provides abundant storage, including an overhead pot rack. The large granite work surface features a lower counter that allows the children to assist in food preparation in safety and comfort.

A secondary island, designed for cleanup, has a raised counter for adult seating that works equally well as a breakfast bar or as a place for guests to enjoy the many sights, smells, and pleasures of cooking. The dining area, which easily seats eight, is surrounded on three sides by furniture-style, rustic pine cabinets for dishware and linens. A crafts center, with its own table and a deep farm sink, also holds an undercounter refrigerator to help feed any starving artists (or children) who happen by. And a desk/office area (not shown) allows Mom to plan household activities while still spending time with the family.

The beauty of this highly functional design is augmented by the orientation of the space. Open to the rear of the house, it provides a spectacular view of the swimming pool, tennis court, and lake.

OPPOSITE AND ABOVE
Design: Joan DesCombes

Architect Andre Rothblatt used clean lines and a neutral palette in this design for a young, very active family. Husband and wife both love to cook, so the space was outfitted with a double set of appliances. And for a child who likes to play, there's plenty of room for fun.

Radiating from the round dining counter is the main cleanup area with a sink and two dishwashers. The counter then cuts a right angle to the stove and "three-car" appliance garage. Nearby is a workstation with a prep sink, dishwasher, and storage drawers. The recessed vertical message center keeps the phone and calendar within easy reach while hiding piles of papers and phone books.

A book-lined family room is also incorporated into the kitchen, with a fully equipped media center in a recess once occupied by a fireplace.

Stainless steel, concrete, curly maple, birch, and a touch of slate bring mellow contrast to all the noise and activity for which this kitchen was built.

OPPOSITE, ABOVE, AND RIGHT
In the play area, window seats make a perfect hiding place for toys and games.
Design: Andre Rothblatt

Secondary Kitchens

With kitchen equipment scaled for any purpose and any space, many of today's homes feature second, and even third, kitchens. Some serve game rooms while others form breakfast bars tucked into a corner or closet of a master suite. A compact snacking kitchen in a home office is another welcome convenience.

Designer Jean Verbridge put an island on wheels in this pool-house kitchen. Fashioned for interaction and flexibility, its easy-care stainless steel top can be used for food prep or as a buffet or dining table. It can be rolled out of the way when things get crowded, and even moved poolside. This is a no-mess, clutter-free space with minimal maintenance required.

This grand outdoor kitchen (opposite) is clearly meant for wining and dining! Designer Joan DesCombes took all her cues from the warm, Florida climate and the gracious hospitality of two home owners who adore celebrating life with friends and family.

BELOW The custom-detailed window molding and island partition add flair to this simple room.
Design: Siemasko + Verbridge

OPPOSITE In a tropical climate an outdoor kitchen may be more important than its indoor rival.
Design: Joan DesCombes

LEFT AND OPPOSITE While many universal kitchen designs include extrawide aisles for wheelchairs, here the aisles have been narrowed to support the home owner, who has difficulty moving about the kitchen or standing for long periods of time. Also, the island is slightly angled to be near to the side-opening ovens in order to make it easier and safer to remove hot pots and pans. Corner-placed appliances, together with a vessel sink on the island, augment the functionality of this beautiful kitchen.
Design: Mark T. White

Universal Design

More than any other room in the house, the kitchen holds the greatest potential for fun, because it's here that we *do* the most, *play* the most, and *laugh* the most. Access is everything, and there should never be any spot in the kitchen that frustrates or impedes us — whether we're eight or eighty-eight, agile or fragile. This is what universal design is all about. The term is often used to refer to design that accommodates individuals who use wheelchairs or are otherwise restricted. But increasingly, universal design is used in a broader sense to refer to design that gracefully accommodates all of us as we move through life.

We are discovering that conveniences created for the uniquely challenged ultimately help each of us. And, as floor plans and furniture placement are reconsidered to accommodate our individual needs, our sense of functional style is also being reexamined.

We realize that a wider passage gracefully opens traffic patterns, and that beauty in the kitchen is only achieved when form truly functions. We are learning that multiple workstations accommodating every member of the family build independence and group spirit at the same time. We are recognizing that, from time to time, some of us who share the same kitchen may become dependent on technology for executing daily chores.

Wishing to stay in our own homes for as long as possible as we age, we are beginning to develop a forward-thinking design sensibility. Our universal consciousness is awakening.

Final Thoughts

I cannot overemphasize how crucial it is, during this stage in the kitchen-design process, to think freely. Function is do*ing,* so brainstorm by imagining every "ing" word you can think of. Throw away any kitchen preconceptions that are holding you down and *think action.* Be specific. Instead of a generic idea such as cooking, say searing, poaching, or deep-frying. Don't say hobbies (or chores), say potting or painting or grooming the pets.

In short, give yourself permission to explore every functional idea you can think of that will turn your new kitchen into a room that really works for you.

All kitchen magic begins with space and light — our two greatest design luxuries.

architecture — the three-dimensional volume of space and light that is sculpted with walls, ceilings, floors, partitions, doors, archways, windows, and skylights — is the single most important element of any kitchen design. Equal parts solid and empty, earth and air. Though our eye may be attracted to color, or dazzled by state-of-the-art appliances, the fundamental power of a kitchen design derives from its architecture.

Our bodies respond instinctively to every interior we enter. With good architecture, a large space can embrace and shelter us, and even the smallest of rooms can present itself with dignity and importance.

If the architecture is right, modest materials can seem rich. But if the architecture is flawed, the visual and emotional impact of the finest materials will be blunted.

ABOVE A massive lintel — floating above a professional-style range, large copper pots, and a farm sink — brings a sense of stature to a tiny kitchen.
Design: Mick De Giulio

OPPOSITE A grand arch of double-tiered windows adds even more sunshine to this warm, luxurious family kitchen.
Design: Marcus Gleysteen

raw space

When faced with a choice of investing in either architecture or materials and appliances, you would be wise in most cases to choose the former. Architecture will have a greater impact on your kitchen design, and you can always upgrade materials and appliances later.

Chapter eight discussed how your new kitchen should function. Now it's time to consider the shape of your kitchen, making sure that it not only accommodates all of the functional elements you desire but also conveys the feeling you want. This process — which applies to remodeling as well as new construction projects — involves examining space and light, and manipulating these precious "immaterial materials" to sculpt your kitchen in the best possible way.

If the space available for your new kitchen feels too small, think about ways to enlarge it. Many home owners assume that the raw space for their new design is predetermined by the old design. But this is where the real breakthrough thinking can occur.

You can enlarge the space by borrowing *horizontally* from other rooms, or *vertically* from attics or basements. And as we shall see later in this chapter, sometimes you can simply pick your kitchen up and move it to a new location!

Changing the architecture of a ceiling can profoundly alter the feeling of a room. For example, adjoining rooms with slightly different ceiling heights can be visually unsettling. Making the ceilings all the same height can bring harmony to disparate spaces. On the other hand, in an open plan, contrasting ceiling styles and heights may actually help to define separate areas. Raising the ceiling even a foot can make a room seem far more spacious. And coffers, vaults, or beams add dimension and texture, completely altering a room's visual impact.

Floors can also significantly affect the feeling of a room by defining the space in a very conscious way. Floor coverings that end at the doors to your kitchen may create a visual boundary while a flooring material that continues into the adjacent rooms, or changes a few feet *before* the door, can underscore a feeling of openness and flow, pulling you from one room into another. Simply laying floor tiles in a diagonal grid can also make a room seem larger. (See below.) And like ceilings, floors can be raised or lowered to define spaces and create visual impact.

Sometimes a feeling of spaciousness can be created by eliminating kitchen walls partially or altogether, and defining the space in more subtle ways, such as with half walls, archways, and partitions.

ABOVE In this open plan, the high-tech stainless steel kitchen is defined by an inset, highly polished black granite floor. The aged and sturdy butcher-block table, posted like a sentry at the corner, not only provides texture and contrast but functions almost as a pillar, architecturally reinforcing the boundary of the kitchen.
Design: Yves-Claude

RIGHT By merely painting an old wood floor with a bold black-and-white checkerboard pattern on a diagonal axis and omitting window treatments from the French doors, the architect transforms this city kitchen into a study in light and unimpeded space.
Design: Duckham + McDougal Architects

When designing your raw space, consider adding a pantry. Whether it's used as a passageway, a utility closet, or a small room unto itself, a pantry will free up space in your kitchen by providing storage and accommodating other functions such as housing small appliances, an extra dishwasher, a wet bar, or even a self-contained cleanup station.

ABOVE In this visually open pantry, a prep island becomes a wall. The two-sided glass-front cabinets above serve as windows, neatly separating the functional and storage areas from the social center of this busy family space.
Design: Stuart Cohen & Julie Hacker Architects and Jennifer Morgenstern

ABOVE RIGHT In this small back pantry that serves as a passageway between the kitchen and dining room, the original mahogany countertop — and even an old radiator — bring authentic, historic charm to this lovely home.
Design: Cameron Snyder

If physically expanding your kitchen isn't an option, think about how you can create the illusion of more space. One of the best ways is with light.

Architecture is not defined by solid forms alone. Light and shadow play a crucial role in our perception of space. The success of a kitchen design depends to a large extent on the proper relationship between light (both natural and artificial) and the solid architectural frame of your room. Without the play of light and shadow, curves flatten out, rich details are obscured, and solid shapes can virtually disappear.

Windows and skylights are the most obvious ways to bring in natural light, but there are countless exciting variations that add architectural richness as well. Clerestory, conservatory, and porthole windows; stained- or art-glass windows; French doors; and transparent or translucent panels and doors are among the options.

RIGHT Double glazing turns this custom cabinet of wood-grained laminate and steel into a window that lets sun shine in and offers a garden view. At night, privacy is provided by a shade behind the cabinet while built-in lighting plays over multicolored dishware, creating the effect of a stained-glass light box.
Design: O. Franco Nonahal

BELOW This architectural treatment brings natural light inside while maintaining a sheltering privacy from nearby houses. A row of clerestory windows was built above the cabinets, with two narrow, peekaboo windows just over the counter.
Design: Roger N. Goldstein

LEFT   Double ovens? Well, not exactly . . . it's the old mirror trick. The illusion of space and light can be almost as uplifting as the real thing.
Design: Gary and Marty Matson

Artificial light is essential when natural light is not available. Therefore, pay careful attention to the selection and placement of general, task, and accent lights. Chandeliers, lamps, and sconces, as well as track, recessed, and concealed cove lighting — or even faux windows and skylights — are just some of the choices available to you.

Reflective surfaces such as mirrors, highly polished metals and stones, and glossy ceramics, as well as more subtly reflective surfaces such as satin-finished stainless steel and copper, can augment both light and space.

OPPOSITE   Sometimes the "room with a view" is just beyond the kitchen. The solution here is a classic arched pass-through that not only captures the magnificent ocean vista but transforms the entire experience of the room.
Design: Mark T. White

RIGHT   Here, the search for space led to an unused attic that was then converted into a family library. By opening up the attic wall to the kitchen, and visually incorporating the skylight and the outline of the stepped bookcase, the designer allows the upper space of this highly geometric kitchen to become as important to the design as the well-grounded lower spaces.
Design: Mojo Stumer Associates

BELOW Sitting next to its modern counterpart, a Colonial-style fireplace is the defining feature of this hardworking country kitchen. Massive and full of character, it anchors the room with history.
Design: Scott Salvator

RIGHT AND BOTTOM RIGHT Designed on one side with a custom stainless attachment for wood grilling, this double-sided fireplace pivots at forty-five degrees from the main kitchen area to open onto the adjoining octagonal breakfast room. Occupying a dominant position in the room, the fire pit becomes the focal point, calling for only the simplest detailing: a green slate mantel, flush slate hearths, and modest recesses for firewood.
Design: Adolfo Perez

Fireplaces — both wood-burning and gas — also provide an excellent way of adding light as well as architectural interest. They may no longer be necessary for heating or cooking, but their aesthetic power to anchor the design of any room remains undiminished.

Because the architectural shell you are creating will have a permanent impact on every other design decision you make, there are two important rules to remember:

First, think contextually. Before any sinks, stoves, or refrigerators are installed, the empty room itself should be designed within the context of the spaces around it — your home, the land, and the region in which you live. Designing the raw space of your kitchen is not only about the feeling you have when you are in the space but about how you feel as you pass through it into other rooms and out-of-doors.

Second, give yourself all the time you need to explore and evaluate every spatial option available, in an unhurried way, and with an inch-by-inch attention to detail. The most visionary ideas for your design will inevitably grow from this early scrutiny of your existing kitchen and its adjoining spaces.

BELOW Floating above the floor, this custom-designed screen of steel and sandblasted glass — detailed with simple, mullionlike rods — serves as an oversize window/door that expands the space and increases the light between the kitchen and its adjoining dining room.
Design: Fu-Tung Cheng

Each of the four kitchens you're about to tour demonstrates how space and light can be effectively modeled to suit the complex practical and aesthetic needs of today's kitchen.

The kitchen shown here is a wonderful example of breakthrough thinking about raw space. It was created by designer Jean Verbridge, who loves to tell her clients, "When you have a choice between 'stuff' and 'space,' always choose space." The original kitchen in this turn-of-the-century Victorian summer residence was a small, dark room at the front of the house with a single window facing the road (rather than the ocean, which was visible from the back of

the home). The design challenge was formidable: to create a new, light-filled kitchen with more room for friends and family gatherings that would look as if it were built almost 100 years ago — a kitchen that would relate gracefully to the rest of the house and accommodate all the functional requirements of a busy modern family.

After examining the original kitchen as well as all the adjacent spaces, Verbridge made a radical suggestion: Why not move the whole kitchen to the back of the house, into the area previously occupied by a wraparound porch and the dining/sitting room? And that's precisely what she did!

This panoramic kitchen (including an open family room with its original fireplace, dining area, workstation, and easy access to the outdoors) has brought a whole new orientation to the architecture of this home. The feeling of protected privacy that came with placing the kitchen away from the front road is enhanced by an unobstructed view of the ocean. This is not just a new kitchen; it's a new experience.

To bring the outside in, double-hung windows with transoms were wrapped around the kitchen in lieu of upper cabinets. With the light pouring in, mornings in this kitchen are absolutely inspirational.

To allay the clients' initial concern that having no upper cabinets would mean insufficient storage, large roll-out drawers were included in the lower cabinets, and a center island and two pantries were added to the plan. Of special interest is the "dirty pantry," with a pocket door that closes to hide the little messes of daily life. Notice that the single upper cabinet in the corner is glazed, with a shelf above that keeps this design as open as possible.

In the dining area, defined by the coffered ceiling and the window seats, the flow of space remains uninterrupted and the classic simplicity of the styling is maintained.

OPPOSITE, ABOVE, AND RIGHT
A built-in desk turns an unused corridor into an important workstation.
Design: Jean Verbridge

The design of this kitchen in a new custom-built house in California is a vivid illustration of how kitchen architecture has changed with our lifestyles over the last several decades. Tackling the issues of a narrow lot and the complex needs of a modern family, architects Leo Marmol and Ron Radziner created this unique light-drenched kitchen atrium that serves as the home's main entryway, central gathering space, and architectural core.

At the front door, a staircase rises dramatically to a mezzanine. At the same time, the compressed lower space elicits curiosity, immediately pulling the eye around the corner and into the open volume of the kitchen. The recessed center skylight, shaded with its trellislike structure constructed of Douglas fir, expands the space skyward.

ABOVE AND OPPOSITE
Design: Marmol Radziner + Associates

Defined by a steel-and-wire-mesh railing system, the open library/hallway develops the space vertically as well, and the panoply of books adds not only color and texture but an intimation of the people who live here. The kitchen sits at the nexus of the living room, dining room, and family room, and is conveniently located next to the laundry room.

True to its context, this kitchen, with a redwood deck outside and a view of the treetops through the skylight, supports an active and ongoing exchange between interior and exterior space.

Some new kitchens blend gently into the home; others challenge and enhance the architectural and natural beauty that surround them. That's certainly the case with this kitchen, designed by architect Adolfo Perez.

Faced with the creative opportunity to construct a new kitchen in this contemporary glass-and-stone house — sitting proudly atop a rugged cliff with spectacular views of the Atlantic Ocean — Perez designed the kitchen space without walls.

While taking cues from the original structure, Perez added his own signature and a heightened sense of drama to the entire main floor. Subtle new forms and materials announce a fresh point of view.

Perched dramatically above the living room like a house within a house, the freestanding architecture of this kitchen echoes the bold volumetric design of the home, rendered in substantial natural materials. The abstract planes above the counters reference the curves of this unique residence and add a sense of power and velocity to the design, as do the strong vertical elements: the pendant lights and the three red copper posts that support the cantilevered roof.

The fine woodwork that frames the kitchen's exterior becomes a run of highly functional base cabinets on the interior, providing all necessary storage and accommodating a compact and efficient work triangle. And with no walls, the space seems boundless.

OPPOSITE AND ABOVE
Design: Adolfo Perez

Designer Deborah Timmermann planned the new kitchen shown below to be large enough to accommodate all the modern bells and whistles while still ringing true to its historic context.

Adhering to the strict guidelines set by the Historic District Commission on Nantucket Island, this kitchen addition, in the style of an old milk barn, was built to provide enough raw space for the many functions required. From the outside, the small peaked-roof farm building looks as if it might have been relocated from some other site and added onto the main house, growing piecemeal like so many other homes in the area. On the inside, this authenticity is reinforced by painstaking attention to detail and by the use of antiques and recycled materials that date back more than a century.

A vaulted ceiling following the roofline, and featuring huge 150-year-old chestnut beams taken from an old barn in Massachusetts, doubles the volume of the space, transforming the beautiful into the extraordinary. (Try covering the top of the image opposite with your hand to see the full impact of this ceiling architecture.)

The delicate balance between old-fashioned styling and contemporary engineering is apparent in the rough pine planks and exposed rafters that hide a modern, insulated roof structure. Above the beam line, recessed lighting works in tandem with a rewired oil-burning schoolhouse chandelier to emphasize the exhilarating verticality of the pitched roof. The antique columns supporting the center island are a subtle reference to what might have been a doorway between the kitchen and dining room. Today, it is the island itself that becomes the architectural divider.

A tiny hayloftlike space above the sitting area and three small adjoining areas (guest room, laundry, and pantry) complete the functional requirements for this active family.

The architectural focal point in the dining area is the unembellished brick fireplace, with a quirky, primitive design that adds a soulful tinge to the warm-and-worn tone of this brand-new old-fashioned kitchen.

Final Thoughts

Fundamentally, your kitchen consists of six elevations: four walls, a floor, and a ceiling. Examine each carefully. Think outside of that standard kitchen box in order to maximize the potential of your design. Consider soaring diagonals, portals, arches, columns, niches, and other dramatic compressions and expansions of space. Add a fireplace, introduce a dormer or conservatory window, raise a ceiling or lower a floor, add a staircase or remove one. Determine whether you prefer a room punctuated with niches and nooks, alcoves or bays, or one with a more austere delineation of line and form.

The architectural shell you create for your new kitchen will prove to be the most enduring of all the elements of your design. It will accommodate and enhance all your other plans and dreams by means of its all-enabling and quiet power.

LEFT AND OPPOSITE
Design: Deborah H. Timmermann

The story of today's kitchen
floor plan begins "Once upon a time,
there was a little triangle . . ."

ABOVE AND OPPOSITE Prep
stations and breakfast bars can
complement the main work triangle
in traditional or modern kitchens.
Design: Pete Giorgi and Ellen Cheever [above],
Adolfo Perez [opposite]

now that you have decided how you want your kitchen to

perform and have built and lit the stage for it, it's time to

put all the pieces of the set into place. The challenge is to

organize appliances, cabinets, and furniture into groupings

that make your work as easy as possible by eliminating

unnecessary walking, while at the same time providing a

smooth flow of traffic in and through the room.

Whether you're planning a compact kitchen or one

with multiple workstations, it helps to begin with the

time-tested concept of the kitchen triangle: the three

imaginary lines that link your sink, stove, and refrigerator.

The logic is simple and grounded in common sense: To

maximize comfort and convenience, place your appliances

fairly close together, but with enough space in between

for ample work surfaces.

ten

floor plan

Kitchen geometry has become more complicated as we have expanded our kitchens to include multiple work-stations and social areas, and have added so much new technology to support how we work and play there. In addition to the primary cooking and cleanup stations, there can be secondary stations for food prep, baking, grilling, breakfast, laundry, crafts and games, homework, computers, potting, pet grooming, wet bars, and even snacking, as well as family gathering areas, home entertainment centers, kitchen offices, and private reading nooks. Kitchen floor plans can range from one-wall galley kitchens and two-wall corridor kitchens to L-shaped, U-shaped, G-shaped, and even spiral-shaped kitchens, as well as hub kitchens from which other rooms radiate. In the process, our classic kitchen triangle has become elongated, flattened, and stretched into other shapes. But through it all, the philosophy behind the triangle — arranging your appliances, cabinets, and furniture in a way that maximizes your comfort and convenience within the space you have — remains timeless.

ABOVE   Multiple islands floating in this vast, light-filled kitchen graciously separate busy work-stations from the more social areas. The well-planned traffic patterns accommodate small groups as well as large parties.
Design: Stuart Cohen & Julie Hacker Architects and Christine H. Bakalar Designs

RIGHT   A broad arch (a motif repeated in the hearth, in recesses above the cabinets, and in the glazed cabinet doors) provides a panoramic view into this lovely, formal kitchen with center island. Note how the peninsula defines the space, controls access, and provides additional seating and function without compromising the sense of openness.
Design: Joan DesCombes

OPPOSITE   Islands offer endless opportunities for flexible design work, both aesthetically and functionally. The unusual shape of this work/storage/breakfast island was derived from the unusual shape of the kitchen.
Design: Marmol Radziner + Associates

Here is a checklist of ideas to keep in mind as you "floor plan":

➤ **The configuration of your existing space,** as well as the locations of your fuel and electrical sources, will influence and may even dictate your floor plan. Generally most electrical wiring and plumbing can be easily rerouted, but moving wastewater drains and outside vents can be an expensive operation. Consider such moves cautiously, keeping your budget in mind. Leaving things as they are is often the way to go. But sometimes a seemingly wild extravagance — such as moving a gas range across the room — can be the idea that totally transforms a kitchen.

➤ **We can learn a lot from professional chefs.** To maximize convenience and efficiency, they like to stand in one place as much as possible — with their tools and equipment, a water supply, and appropriate waste disposal all in sight and within easy reach — so that they can pivot rather than walk. Ideally, all working chefs have their own self-contained space so that they don't get in one another's way. Also, they like the functional elements to be arranged in a logical pattern so that the food moves smoothly in one direction — from storage, to food prep, to cooking, and then to serving. These ideas can be adapted to your kitchen. For example, having all your storage — both dry and cold — in the same area makes unloading groceries easier and simplifies food preparation. Even incorporating just a small garbage can and roll of paper towels in your secondary prep sink can save you many extra steps.

➤ **Multiple workstations** allow for autonomy and flexibility. But remember, you must provide sufficient floor space for good circulation around the room. In other words, don't overstuff your floor plan.

➤ **With all the new, smaller appliances** available — dishwasher and refrigerator drawers; modular grills and griddles; gas, electric, and steam cooking elements — floor planning is a more flexible process than ever before. Now it's easier

to create independent workstations, custom designed to your own needs. You may want a refrigerator drawer next to the kitchen desk for your bottled water, or your kids might like an area of their own — within easy reach of the lower cabinets — with a microwave and freezer drawer for after-school frozen pizzas. I once saw a kitchen with three separate minicleanup stations, each comprised of a cabinet and dishwasher drawer — one for pots and pans, one for fine china and crystal, and one for everyday dishes.

➤ **Islands have changed kitchen geography forever.** No longer are we confined to the counter, or forced to commandeer the kitchen table when it's time to roll dough or stuff a twenty-pound turkey. When it comes to devising a floor plan, islands offer great opportunities. Accessible from every side, they help minimize congestion. And whether designed for prep work, cooking, or dining, or simply for storage, islands free up wall space, allowing you to open the kitchen to other rooms, or install a window and link your world to the outdoors.

ABOVE   It may be just a ray of
yellow sunshine that streams across
the kitchen table, a peek into your
backyard garden, or a view as
spectacular as these Colorado
mountains — in any form, the
endless energy and variety of nature
are sure to enhance every moment
you spend in your new kitchen.
Design: Ricki Brown

➤ **Wheels on a table or island,** or even a foldaway cart, can
turn a good floor plan into an even better one by giving
you the flexibility to rearrange your layout easily as your
needs change from hour to hour and day to day.

➤ **When space is at a premium,** consider changing a kitchen
island into a peninsula by turning the empty space between
the island and the wall into a cabinet. The traffic pattern may
be a bit more limited, but the trade-off is extra storage space.

- **The placement of your primary sink** is one of the most important decisions you'll make when designing your floor plan. That's where you'll spend most of your time, so select a spot that offers something special to look at. Take advantage of the best view at hand, whether it's an awesome mountain range, a vibrant cityscape, or just a simple flower box. If keeping an eye on the kids is important, consider the relationship of your sink to their indoor play area, the yard, or the place where they do their homework.

- **The least-loved kitchen chore** is doing the dishes, so anything that makes that task easier is worth considering. Multiple dishwashers or dishwasher drawers might be the answer. Cabinets that open from both the "sink side" and the "dining side" make it easier to unload the dishwasher and set the table. Pass-throughs help speed things up too. And a music system or TV set nearby can also make cleanup a lot less tiresome. By the way, be sure to locate dishwashers right next to the sink to avoid dripping water on the floor.

- **Cabinets are for style, storage, and shaping space.** We'll discuss style in chapter eleven, but now's the time for analyzing your storage needs as well as how to configure your cabinets to create the best possible floor plan.

- **A detailed inventory of every item** — everything — in your kitchen will help your floor planning immensely. Armed with this specific information, you'll be able to plan your new storage space with an enlightened perspective on what you have, what you use, and where it has to be. You won't have to guess about the number of drawers you'll need next to the sink, or the proper dimensions for your spice cabinet. This is also a great time to decide whether or not you need to allocate valuable cabinet space to that rice steamer your sister gave you for your first anniversary. (Here's a tip for getting a fresh start in your new kitchen: Saying good-bye to objects with sentimental value, from small things to large pieces of furniture, can be difficult. Consider saving them in a memory book, with snapshots and descriptions of the memories they hold, and then passing the real objects along to a friend, relative, or worthy charity.)

- **Cabinetry needn't simply run along a wall.** It can fill a corner, jut out to form a peninsula, or sit in the center of the kitchen as an island. Explore every option. Peninsulas and islands often function as interior architectural elements to divide rooms or areas within rooms. They can be fashioned to harmonize with the rest of your cabinetry, or designed to offer an eye-catching contrast.

- **If you use your stovetop more than your oven,** consider tucking the oven in an inconspicuous or secondary location.

- **Countertops are invaluable** next to large appliances — a "must" near sinks for prep and dishwashing and indispensable adjacent to ovens and cooktops for handling hot pots and pans. They are equally practical next to cold and dry storage areas; after all, unloading groceries is hard work, so why lug things any farther than you need to? And a long, uninterrupted run of countertop is a wonderful kitchen luxury that can serve many purposes, from laying out a holiday buffet to wrapping birthday presents.

- **Do you want to include your family computer** on a workstation in the kitchen so that you can help your kids with their homework as well as monitor what's on the screen? If so, proper placement of the computer is critical.

- **Think about the kind of seating you want** in your kitchen. Even though most cooking and food preparation is done while standing, knowing where to place your dining chairs, benches, stools, banquettes, and even couches and side chairs can dramatically affect the way that you, your friends, and your family enjoy the new room. Do you want your kitchen to be one that people visit in passing or one in which they set up camp?

- **Make sure that your recycling bins** are conveniently located, and that every workstation has the waste disposal it needs. Trash cans on wheels are practical, and waste chutes to outdoor compost piles make great sense too.

ABOVE With accessible storage below and an exhaust hood suspended from the ceiling, the hearth, set into a peninsula, helps to define the floor plan by separating the social and work areas of this modern kitchen. The seemingly spontaneous combination of mirror finishes, open shelves, and utensils is bursting with enthusiasm for cooking, life, and style.
Design: Maxine Snider

➤ **Floor plans are about style as well as function.** First impressions are critical, so think about the sight lines you are creating from every point of entry. A pleasing view into the room sets the right tone in welcoming friends and family.

➤ **Use every kitchen corner.** If your cabinets meet at the corner of your room, take advantage of the wide variety of revolving and pivoting mechanisms that make all the inside corner space accessible. Placing sinks and other appliances in corners is an effective use of space that can also soften the profile of your floor plan.

➤ **If you are not planning to tear down walls** or otherwise rebuild the raw space of your existing kitchen, here are a few options that may help you enhance the dynamics of your floor plan:

◎ **Employ architectural elements,** such as columns and arches, to separate spaces or open them up to each other.

◎ **Use furniture groupings** to define areas within your floor plan.

◎ **Change the flooring material** or use area rugs to visually partition the space.

◎ **Suspend from the ceiling** — over a table or island — a row of pendant lights, a shelf, or a glazed cabinet to visually separate two areas.

◎ **Whether it is integrated into the decor** of the ceiling architecture or becomes a contrasting sculptural element, an exhaust system hung from the ceiling over a cooktop can also clearly separate different kitchen areas.

➤ **While you may not presently have any special needs** (such as wheelchair accessibility), it doesn't hurt to consider such an eventuality as you plan. There may come a time when the wider aisles and other accommodating spaces you build today will be cherished for more than just their aesthetic appeal.

Here are some examples of kitchen floor plans, in a variety of styles, that achieve compatibility between form and function. Remember, large or small, every kitchen is built one workstation at a time.

With its sweeping, arched entryway and sunshine pouring in from a wall of windows over the sink, this kitchen, designed by Gerard Ciccarello, has assumed a grandeur appropriate to the rest of the new home in which it was built — even though it is only 7' deep!

Light and a sense of space were of paramount importance in this design, so only a few upper cabinets were included. The center island, topped with rich, antique chestnut wood, provides additional storage. The ovens and a wet bar were incorporated into the interior structure of the double arch, and an integrated refrigerator on the right side of the kitchen counterbalances the built-in cooking area on the left. The hearth, with a hidden exhaust hood, is detailed with a handsome fireplace mantel and bright yellow tiles that add more sunshine to the kitchen.

This fanciful family kitchen, designed by Carrie Anne Deane, is also a serious workplace. While there is whimsy in the "found" objects (the old screen door on the pantry and the supermarket sign used as a cap molding on the stairwell) and the open display of tableware and foodstuffs appears casual, a no-nonsense floor plan makes possible the free-flowing asymmetry of all these visual pleasures.

The cleanup area, with drain boards carved into the granite countertops, two 10" deep sinks, two dishwasher drawers, and a professional power nozzle, is centrally located under the kitchen window, just a pivot away from the main cooking station with its four gas burners, barbecue grill, dedicated wok burner, and deep fryer.

The simplicity of the monolithic stainless steel hood and the stainless steel pendant lamps plays against the complexity of the island below, with its raised breakfast bar, dual workstations, and desk.

Wrapped around the end of the island, near the prep sink, is an area for both cold storage and dry goods. Located conveniently near the kitchen's back door and close to the garage, it's *the* spot for unloading groceries.

OPPOSITE, LEFT, AND ABOVE This is a room filled with surfaces and objects that dazzle the eye and pique our curiosity. But just beneath these delightful surfaces, a lot of thoughtful planning is hard at work every day.
Design: Carrie Anne Deane

It is always a challenge to update a kitchen in a home as architecturally significant as this 1950s Usonian house by Frank Lloyd Wright. Here, architect John C. Senhauser took great care to respect the work of this modern master while still meeting the needs of today's family.

The materials used in the remodeled kitchen spring from Wright's original plan: warm cypress wood, stainless steel, soft brass, and red-granule terrazzo. The linearity of the new center island echoes the horizontal motif of the home, including the long ribbon of windows, the projecting cornice above (with its inset lights), and the line of molding under the top row of drawers. The new design also respects the 4' x 4' grid upon which the entire home was patterned (part of Wright's attempt to create an affordable, easily replicated housing design).

The function and the floor plan, however, have been thoughtfully readjusted. Gone are the washer and dryer that once sat on the wall across from the windows. Both the original sink and a peninsula that jutted into the space have been

eliminated. A recess in the chimney that held the original ovens is also gone. The room's new floor plan makes for smooth traffic flow and enhances the cooking and dining experience.

With the cooktop and stainless steel counters flanked by two new ovens and a modern refrigerator that fits perfectly under the original ceiling cornice, the cook in this family has dominion over the workstation; guests, kids, and the dog can easily move around the room without interrupting the work being done across the island. The double sink in the island and a dishwasher that disappears behind cabinetry stained to match the original millwork complete the prep and cleanup station.

Through delicate readjustment of the dimensions of the cabinets near the original secondary sink, this area now serves as both a wet bar and a convenient service pantry for the formal dining room, which is accessed through the door to the left of the wall ovens.

OPPOSITE, ABOVE, AND RIGHT This remodeling has reoriented the kitchen to take best advantage of its expansive views, while also gracefully heightening the function of a classic kitchen that still honors its beautiful heritage.
Design: John C. Senhauser

Gently curved, and dressed in distressed, amber-
colored pine, this warm grouping of spaces — designed
for easy comfort and casual family gatherings by Joan
DesCombes — softly wraps itself around an irregularly
shaped, hand-painted island; pours past a breakfast counter
to embrace a dining area; and comes to rest in an adjoining
family room. The spiraling effect is underscored by the
main cooking station and storage hutch — both set on
angles — and echoed in the curves of the antique pine
corbels supporting the mantel over the hearth, in the recess
above the mantel, and in the spiraling ironwork of the pot
rack. The floor plan accommodates multiple cooks and
kitchen helpers and also provides a perfect perch for family
and guests at the breakfast bar.

OPPOSITE, BELOW, AND RIGHT
Antique wood beams, French terra-cotta flooring, granite counters, and a mix of textiles and painted finishes add to the easy charm that turns a large and highly functional space into a cozy spot for nesting.
Design: Joan DesCombes

Sitting quietly next to a garden — in an open
floor plan shared with a library and living room in a studio
designed for contemplation and study by architects Leo
Marmol and Ron Radziner — a shallow, U-shaped module
of cabinetry results in a kitchen with a strong presence
through the use of just a few simple design elements. In a
neutral palette of natural maple and stainless steel, a one-wall
galley becomes a kitchen in a niche that is formed by a built-
in refrigerator at one end and an open case of shelves, filled
with an assortment of tea cups and pots, at the other end.
The long work surface that runs between them holds the
cooking and cleanup stations. Two tables — one at working
height, the other for sitting — complete the functional
elements of the plan.

OPPOSITE AND ABOVE In this beautiful design, a pure rectangle of raw space has been endowed with a stature beyond its modest scale by means of precision detailing and a vision of elegant restraint.
Design: Marmol Radziner + Associates

OPPOSITE AND ABOVE Highly polished finishes and hot-yellow cabinetry set a theatrical tone in this open kitchen designed by architects Will Ruhl and Brad Walker. But the real drama of the floor plan lies just beyond the sleek granite surface of the slender island, on the wall that opposes the galley. Here, an illuminated floor-to-ceiling translucent "window wall" pivots wide-open to reveal an unexpected secret: a fully equipped home office. When needed, the island and dining table are transformed into desks and the kitchen gets down to business.
Design: Ruhl Walker Architects

Final Thoughts

Every design needs room for real life. No kitchen design is truly complete until it is tested and retested by the life you live in it. No matter how well you may have solved the problems of your old kitchen with a new and improved floor plan, or how clearly you may have visualized yourself working in this reordered space, be prepared for some period of adjustment as you and your new kitchen get acquainted. This is a breaking-in period, a time for some experimentation and small changes to gain a sense of mastery in your new room.

Only after you've served fifty breakfasts, made tea for two at least twice, and had the whole family over for a big holiday dinner will you know the "ins and outs" of your new kitchen. Only after those inevitable first scratches and stains, and the first time the oatmeal boils over onto the cooktop, will you begin to really settle down into the reality of life in your new kitchen. And actually, that's when the fun really begins.

Style has become lifestyle – the second half of how we live.

Whether it's haute couture, ready-to-wear, or do-it-yourself, kitchen style, like fashion, is all about materials and tailoring. Each material you select makes a unique contribution in spirit, character, color, and texture. The way these materials are detailed and combined will define the style of your new kitchen.

For all the surface appeal a well-designed kitchen affords, its beauty is not only skin-deep. Kitchen walls, with their cabinets, countertops, and appliances, are living walls, alive with function — opening generously to serve our needs, then retreating quietly until we beckon them again. There is intelligence, technology, and purpose behind the beauty of every successful kitchen design, a depth that we must not overlook even now, as we examine the stylish surfaces.

ABOVE AND OPPOSITE
This kitchen may virtually disappear when the cabinets close, but the style will definitely endure.
Design: Bruce Bierman Design, Inc.

eleven

style

Your kitchen may draw inspiration from historical American precedents, such as the colonial or federal period, or from contemporary regional styles, such as southwestern. It may take a cue from Tuscany or the charm of French provincial, or range farther afield, borrowing from Asian or African motifs.

When it comes to kitchen style, the menu is multilingual. But like language itself, style is constantly changing. The style that our American forefathers thought of as a contemporary interpretation of European neoclassicism is now called American colonial. The Franklin stove, now considered a charming relic, stirred up tremendous controversy when it was first introduced in the eighteenth century. This "mechanical monster" invading the warm and cozy family kitchens of the time terrified many people.

These days, there is a glorious profusion of kitchen styles, and we have the luxury of being able to choose the one that suits us best. One of the most enjoyable aspects of hosting my TV shows is the pleasure I get from visiting kitchens that are influenced by every period and style.

In a real sense, this chapter is about surfaces. We've already talked about how you will use your new kitchen, how to sculpt the raw space that will hold your kitchen, and how to arrange your appliances and other functional elements within the space. These building blocks of kitchen design will all have an important impact on the style of your kitchen. But whether your new kitchen is traditional, contemporary, or has a look all its own, its *style* will be created primarily by the surfaces of your cabinets, countertops, appliances, walls, windows, floors, and ceilings.

Because cabinets and countertops compose
such a high percentage of the total surfaces in a kitchen, they
generally establish the style of the kitchen. And because many
materials can function successfully in both traditional and
contemporary formats, the style of your kitchen will depend
less upon what materials are used than on how they are fabricated and combined.

ABOVE In a kitchen designed to
blend seamlessly with surrounding
rooms rather than to make a
statement of its own, a sensitive
palette of materials — back-painted
tempered glass, Carrara marble,
Swiss pear wood, and polished
chrome — creates a fluid continuity
with understated elegance.
Design: Emanuela Frattini Magnusson

RIGHT A refreshing juxtaposition
of perforated stainless steel and
polished concrete enhances the
dramatic sweep of this island
countertop.
Design: Fu-Tung Cheng

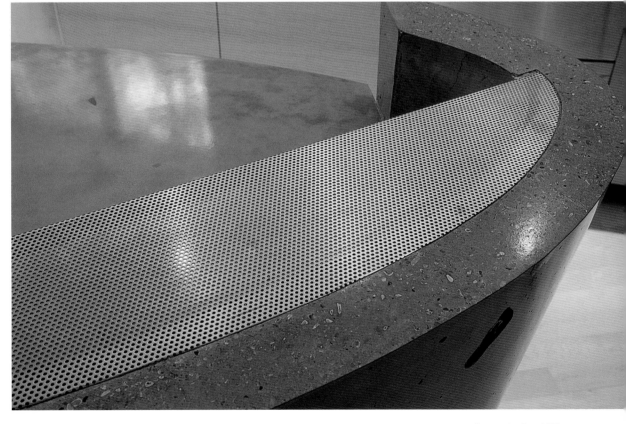

OPPOSITE A huge slab of 6" thick butcher block emphasizes the robust scale of this long and sturdy island. The light wood also makes a complementary contrast to the antiqued, sage-green base.
Design: Ricki Brown

ABOVE AND RIGHT Not so long ago, we would have been surprised to see concrete in the kitchen, but today it is used increasingly for countertops. As these two images show, with good design, this new application can be equally at home in contemporary and traditional styles.
Design: Fu-Tung Cheng [above], Beverly A. Alig [right]

LEFT There is polish and purpose in this contemporary interpretation of the classic American hearth. Now made of steel and glossy black subway tiles, its hearty, welcoming spirit remains unchanged, despite the vast technological revolution of the past century.
Design: Ricki Brown

Here are a few thoughts to keep in mind as you begin window-shopping for your personal kitchen style:

➤ **Kitchen designs often begin with one simple idea:** a dishware pattern, a professional cooktop you've always dreamed of, a favorite color. Arriving at that first idea may be effortless, but in most cases it takes time and effort, like finding a strand of thread in that tiny slot on the top of a spool. But once it's found, your design will unwind before your eyes. There is a logic that connects one design idea to the next. Just follow that little thread.

➤ **Today's kitchens are as finely crafted** and highly refined as any other room in the house, and the style you choose can be as humble or as heightened as you like. Whether you creatively assemble salvaged materials, devise a futuristic space-age machine, or re-create a period room, enjoy the freedom to do things your way! Remember, when friends and family visit, they're coming to see you. So the more there is of *you* in your design, the better.

➤ **Kitchen appliances get fancier every day** (or simpler, depending on your needs and tastes). New technology is redefining function and design in the kitchen; explore all the possibilities before you invest in major appliances.

➤ **Manufacturers have come up with ranges** that cook dinner and then keep it warm until you get home from work, and even refrigerate it if you're late. There are washing machines that know what they're washing, and self-regulate if you've set the wrong cycle. Soon your refrigerator will be ordering groceries from the store before you even realize that you're low on eggs and milk.

➤ **Professional-caliber cooking equipment** is more popular than ever, making a big impact on style as well as function. In fact, many builders and home owners who are thinking about resale are making high-tech ranges and refrigerators a top priority in new kitchens.

➤ **New colors, finishes, and styling** are turning everyday appliances into highly useful works of kitchen art. Choose them for looks as well as function.

➤ **Modular appliances,** appliances designed as drawers, and new options such as tall, skinny, and even round refrigerators make it possible to understand space in totally new ways.

➤ **Ductless ventilation** now allows you to place a cooktop anywhere.

➤ **Hardware details** can have a big impact. Latches, pulls, knobs, and faucets are a wonderful means of self-expression.

➤ **It's no longer a metaphor** to speak about tailoring a kitchen. Cabinets and counters are now being sized according to your own personal measurements, and designed to accommodate all your special needs.

➤ **Clarity of style can be established** with a few strong choices. Selecting a single focal point in your kitchen to express that style is often all it takes!

➤ **Care should be given to entryways,** portals, and all other transitions between rooms. They help establish the feel of a kitchen and make a strong style statement.

➤ **Sight lines are critical.** What catches the eye as you enter a room will make a lasting first impression. Placing a focal point of your design — such as that special hearth — on the wall opposite your doorway can be effective.

➤ **Because we perceive the scale of a room** by what we see at eye level, using open shelves and open expanses of countertops will make your kitchen feel bigger.

➤ **Be realistic.** Assess the pros and cons of each material you choose. For example, natural stones can chip and may need special care. Laminates are more affordable but may be less durable than other materials. Carefully consider the maintenance necessary to preserve the look you love.

ABOVE AND OPPOSITE
Design: Barbara Jacobs

As we examine the kitchens that follow, a good
deal of attention will be paid to the cabinetry, countertops, and
appliances. But as you will see, a well-executed kitchen design
is the result of all the individual forms, masses, materials, and
patterns working together harmoniously.

The colorful styling of the very personal kitchen design
illustrated here begins at the hearth, where designer Barbara
Jacobs brings together her clients' passions for gourmet

cooking and Italian majolica pottery. Above the handsome steel and brass French range (the first item selected) is a custom mosaic backsplash and stepped hood created by San Francisco tile artist Karen Thompson. Displaying the colors and geometric patterns from the majolica collection, this serviceable focal point, along with its fraternal twin — the fireplace hearth at the other end of the space — became the inspiration for the rest of the decor.

The concentric pattern of the kitchen floor centers the room and marks the footprint of the work island and integrated eating area, while the floor boards in the adjoining family room shift into standard parallel formation with a

five-strip border. This attentive detailing continues in the cabinetry. Influenced by the classic simplicity of the Arts and Crafts style, the rather thick stiles and rails are accented with copper-finished wrought iron pulls. The size and scale of the cabinets are skillfully orchestrated to step up gradually toward the dramatic roofline, giving the room a comfortable, human scale.

With its palette of purple, blue, and gold tones against a background of creamy yellow walls, green-black granite countertops, and warm wood cabinets and floors, the room seems to vibrate with energy. It's a happy space for playful children and busy grown-ups alike.

The serenity of this design by Fu-Tung Cheng is embodied in the simple beauty of the Japanese screen floating above the cabinetry in the family seating area. We might easily call this a Zen kitchen; but before we rush to name its style, let's look more closely at the architecture and design of these spaces, for just below the apparent simplicity is a richness of ideas from multiple sources — Asia, Europe, and America.

Recessed in a cove created by a lowered ceiling (in striking contrast to the central ceiling, with its dramatic run of horizontal skylights and delicate pin spotlights), the working walls of the kitchen make a powerful architectural statement.

The visual interest continues with the cabinets, where Cheng has found fresh ways to express function and use materials. The direction of the wood grain shifts from panel

to panel, and one cabinet — the appliance garage — is made of two exotic woods, *anigre* and *mecare*. Shapes are varied and asymmetrical (notice the diagonally cut cabinet door next to the refrigerator and the hardware application). All around the room, layered materials — butcher block, concrete, steel, granite, and plaster — give this design a robust heft. And the unexpected corner fireplace reminds us that this kitchen follows no rules but its own.

Art and technology are seamlessly wedded. High-tech refrigeration and surround sound are right at home with the concrete counter imbedded with turquoise and fossils, and the hand-carved, eggplant-colored plaster sheath over the range hood.

To art historians, this style might recall the prairie vision of Frank Lloyd Wright, the linearity of cubism, or the functional spirit of the German Bauhaus. But rather than peg this kitchen to any specific style, perhaps it's wiser simply to absorb its beauty. You may then be inspired to dream new kitchen dreams all your own.

OPPOSITE, ABOVE, AND RIGHT
Design: Fu-Tung Cheng

This fifth-floor city kitchen takes on the charm and luminescent serenity of Swedish styling. Faced with the urban dilemma of limited daylight, designer Nancy Mullan maximized the available light by borrowing ideas from Scandinavia, where compensating for long months of meager sunshine is an art. The solution — a white kitchen with blue-gray granite countertops and accents of blue — reflects a characteristically soft, Swedish palette. There is far more to these surfaces, however, than initially meets the eye.

With a gentle addition of blue, gray, and violet pigments, Mullan has created multiple whites — whites with shadowed, muted tonalities that bring subtlety and sophistication to the simplicity of this white kitchen design. Interestingly, Mullan says that this deliberate artistic manipulation of color is an idea inspired by nature, for even in an all-white room, every wall takes on its own value as the light changes throughout the day. Her goal was to give nature a helping hand, with more richly modeled surfaces that add visual depth and a

certain moodiness. This feeling is further enriched by multiple layers of faux finishing (wood first stained blue, then painted white, then distressed) that give the cabinets a bit of age and history.

The stone counters are complemented by faux-painted marble on the refrigerator hutch, a trick very much in keeping with the Gustavian Swedish tradition (1770–90) of finding affordable ways to mimic the elegance and grandeur of the French court.

By the way, while it has been said that the Swedish style began as an attempt to *copy*, it is now highly esteemed for its own innate value. So while you may start with someone else's idea, once you have reworked it to fit your personal style and budget, that idea takes on a new and unique identity.

The rustic imperfections of the floor, bleached and pickled to match the decor, also add an aged, antique feeling that harmonizes with the clean, spare lines of the furniture and the gingham and floral textiles that complete the dining area.

According to one Swedish guest, this kitchen "is just like my grandmother's house, only better."

This family kitchen, designed by Barbara Jacobs, takes its style from ancient Japanese aesthetic traditions. Natural materials and clean forms evoke an Asian tranquility, belying the high-tech functions veiled beneath the surfaces.

Intrigued by the multiplicity of patterns in antique wooden *tansu* chests, Jacobs combined five different styles of doors and drawers to bring texture to the quiet uniformity of the wood grain. There are doors detailed with multiple narrow strips of wood set at 3" intervals; flat, flush panels detailed with iron corner trim and center pulls; and recessed panels with raised rails and stiles (some with horizontal centerpieces, some built in pairs to look like a single door). Jacobs integrated the refrigerator/freezer by deftly combining two of these contrasting motifs.

Like pathways of moss in a Japanese garden, long green slabs of granite traverse the warm, clear cherry cabinets. Black accessories, appliances, hardware, and suspended lighting fixtures work with highlights of orange lacquer to further root this design in an authentic Japanese palette.

The delightful finishing touch is an inventive appliance garage, made by the designer herself from a small bamboo screen and lined with Japanese rice paper.

Cowboy-booted barstools set a whimsical tone in this eclectic kitchen created by designer Ricki Brown. The moment you step inside, you know you're here to kick back and have fun.

It all began with the massive antique-copper ventilation hood from an old restaurant, which led to the idea of the hammered copper island countertop, the copper accessories, and the corresponding use of other strong metals (stainless steel and wrought iron) throughout the room. These metallic hues were then partnered with red, black, and natural-pine cabinet finishes for a bold, earthy look.

Smooth oatmeal-colored granite counters with rugged snap edges surround the cleanup and cooking stations while a multicolored slate-tile backsplash rises behind the hearth.

A two-tier wrought iron pot rack and chandelier follows the triangular shape of the island below. The pleasing jumble of pots, pans, and baskets matches the rodeo rhythms of the color, texture, and material that mix together so freely in the lower half of this voluminous, barnlike space.

From the heavy ceiling beams to the variegated antique oak floor, family treasures, "found" objects, and lighthearted good humor make this kitchen a party.

Final Thoughts

Whether it is a restoration, a renovation, or a new construction, your new kitchen can be gorgeous in any style. The beauty will depend less on which style you choose than on the manner in which the elements of it are combined and executed — and, of course, on how well it suits you. That's style!

Fifty years from now, when designers look back on our kitchens, I wonder what they will say. Will kitchen forms and functions have changed markedly? Perhaps kitchens will revert to the small, closed rooms they once were but will be so technologically advanced that they will shop, cook, serve, and (yes!) even clean up after themselves.

What we do know now is that, just around the beginning of the twenty-first century, kitchen styles were abundant and profuse, and each in its own way was an expression of self.

OPPOSITE AND BELOW
Design: Ricki Brown

The fifth building block of kitchen design is you.

as you design your new kitchen, remember that you — your tastes, values, personal history, interests, and personality — are as critically important as any other element of your design. If you let them, these personal qualities will infuse your kitchen design with a spirit all its own.

Here is a collection of nine wonderfully personal kitchens that work beautifully. The first, seen here, was designed by Fu-Tung Cheng for Wendy Roess-DeCenzo, whose adventurous art spirit made this a perfect collaboration.

ABOVE AND OPPOSITE
There is a lovely duality to this kitchen, cozy and grand as well as exciting and serene. Once a painter, Cheng now brings art into his kitchen designs by finding different ways to interpret everyday objects, and then sculpting new forms from function.
Design: Fu-Tung Cheng

twelve

it's my kitchen!

ABOVE AND OPPOSITE The kitchen, oriented eastward toward a patio beyond the curtain-wall windows, also has an intimate relationship with the dining and living spaces that sit just behind it.
Design: Fu-Tung Cheng

Under a cloudlike vault finished in two tones of foggy gray and facing a sunny wall of windows sits a penthouse kitchen by designer Fu-Tung Cheng. With an artistic license issued by his young and sophisticated client, Cheng created a design driven by open volumes of space and an expressive, explorative sense of materiality.

A harmony of neutral tones and natural materials comes alive with unexpected visual surprises. The expansive, raked-plaster ceiling — pierced with a slit of skylight — has the furrowed look of corduroy. Handmade crackled tiles sheath the rear partition, contrasting with the flat gray of the terrazzo floor that is inlayed with rhythmic copper strips and scattered with amazonite and turquoise. The concrete island pulses with integrated red and purple-blue tonalities while wood tones and textures in the bamboo cabinetry, the recycled "street elm" island tabletop, and the glossy surfboard banquette table join with perforated and smooth reflective stainless steel to add even more variety. Honeycombed aluminum between translucent fiberglass sheets floats into the kitchen from a mezzanine above.

The weighty proportions of individual design elements in the kitchen combine to create a feeling of safety, enclosure,

and intimacy without standard walls. The room is literally and figuratively defined by function. Cheng designed a wall-length, stainless rinsing sink and companion soaking sink with dual professional faucets, as well as the 11' hood with outriggers and glass shelves that shelters the kitchen from above. Insetting four modular cooking elements on the center island further customized both the design and the way the kitchen works. A storage pantry, accessed through a door to the left of the stainless utility wall, houses a washer and dryer. The glass wall above the pantry maintains the open flow of space.

A notch in the cream-colored tile wall connects the rooms visually, and one of the two living-room fireplaces, built high enough for cooking, serves as an auxiliary kitchen workstation.

LEFT AND OPPOSITE With its dynamic balancing of space and light, this design achieves a peaceful equilibrium that is both silent and strong.
Design: Brininstool + Lynch

Soon after they moved in, Tom and Nancy
Yamamoto called their architect, Brad Lynch, to express the pleasure of living in their new home. Tom told Brad, "I'm standing in the kitchen in my robe and slippers, and I know that I live in the most beautiful house in the world." According to Tom, this pleasure increases over time, as new subtleties in the design continue to reveal themselves.

The vision for the house began with a desire to display a prize possession: a pair of seventeenth-century *Yamato-e* screens that, for Tom and Nancy, capture the essence of Japanese culture and its reverence for nature. Lynch designed separate, illuminated niches as architectural focal points from which the screens could be enjoyed from all of the open living spaces in the home, including the kitchen.

Intentionally designed with no hierarchy of rooms — "no space subservient to any other" — all the sculptural volumes work together and flow into one another, one room mysteriously drawing you into the next. Because Lynch designs sculp-

turally, there are no apparent beginnings or endings. Inspired by the sculpture of Henry Moore, Lynch seeks to resolve the positive and negative spaces from every perspective.

Using colors, natural materials, and rectilinear shapes that echo the antique screens, Lynch partially enclosed the kitchen within walls of cabinetry, creating a semiprivate work space that is still part of the main dining and entertaining areas. The panoramic view from the sink takes in everything, including the drama of the monolithic fireplace sheathed in aluminum leaf — a modern variation on the gold leaf of the screens.

The appliances are arranged in a simple triangle, with the cooktop on a center island and the ovens and refrigerator framed by maple. With minimal hardware and a rhythmic grid of doors and drawers, the flush overlay cabinet doors reinforce the understated elegance of the entire plan.

To create the effect of natural light in the kitchen, Lynch designed a faux skylight within a metal grid. The grid becomes a framework for mounted lights as it projects over the dining table.

When Marc Thee told kitchen designer Jackie Brown that the kitchen she'd designed was his favorite room in the house, she was elated. After all, Marc and his partner, Michael Abbott — both interior designers — know the importance of pleasing clients, and they've set their own high standards for functionality, craftsmanship, and creativity.

This magical kitchen, alive with contrasts, blends Gothic, Moorish, traditional, and contemporary styles. The design combines the personalities of both home owners within a floor plan that is flexible enough for grand-scale entertaining or a dinner for two. With a formal dining room at one end, the breakfast nook just past the wooden portal, and a small but fully equipped catering kitchen (at left), this design has plenty of space for serving and has seating to spare.

The central hearth, with a granite backsplash, is set in a glistening pattern of off-white, amber, and soft-blue glass tiles, and features a heavy-duty professional range and exhaust hood. The crisp, reflective stainless appliances and cabinets sparkling throughout the room balance the golden granite counters, creamy limestone floors, and hand-painted ceiling beams and rafters.

Complementing the traditional, solid cherry, raised-panel cabinets are cabinets made of solid stainless steel, and others with frames of wood or steel that showcase insets made of layers of glass, perforated stainless steel, and rice paper.

Dominating the main space, a five-story pantry-tower with a movable ladder and pullout shelves provides enough storage for both these kitchens . . . and then some.

OPPOSITE AND RIGHT The clerestory windows, in a Gothic motif, let in natural light through the robin's egg blue sky of the walls, and the entire space is oriented toward a stately courtyard with a koi pond and lake beyond.
Design: Jackie Brown and Marc-Michaels Interior Design, Inc.

Flush cabinet doors and drawers, sized to accommodate the chef's commercial pots and other exacting technical requirements, were set into an abstract black grid to evoke the scheme of Mondrian's paintings. For contrast, Torrell used several doors of black stained maple with ribbed-glass insets. The black laminate countertops with fluted edging match the diner stools at the island.

The vitality of the aesthetic is rivaled by the functional aspects of this design. Old and new modular cooking hobs were combined to suit the chef's cooking style. New appliances were added, including a larger refrigerator and a separate beverage refrigerator. The island was designed to allow the chef easy access to the ample work surfaces, his cooking utensils, and the sink.

Limited by the available footprint that could not accommodate a walk-in pantry, Torrell had to engineer creative solutions for additional storage, using spaces that might easily have been overlooked. The space *inside* the walls was used by

Artist James Ray wanted a new kitchen that both looked like a work by Dutch painter Piet Mondrian and met the exacting technical and practical specifications of Ray's professional chef. For designer Betty Torrell, the challenge was further complicated by Ray's wish to keep the relatively new gray floor and several of the appliances from the existing kitchen, to use multiple metal finishes, and to do it all without altering the existing architectural shell. The result of their collaboration is the wonderful kitchen shown here.

The idea of combining a metallic palette of stainless steel, brass, and copper colors with a Mondrian palette of red, white, and blue (the colors most often associated with his work) presented a bit of an aesthetic dilemma, so Torrell did some research. Luckily she found some early Mondrian drawings in orange, white, and yellow — colors that pleased her client and would mix well with the various metals and the existing gray floor.

recessing a "one-can-deep," floor-to-ceiling pantry between the studs, providing the chef with a view of all the staples inside at a single glance. As an added touch, a tiny wedge of space between the ovens and back door was converted into a closet for dog leashes, keys, and other narrow items. To avoid the need for air-conditioning, Torrell used a ceiling fan in combination with high windows to allow heated air to escape.

The French country kitchen shown here belongs to a young professional couple who wanted a design with a timeless elegance that would complement the architecture of their newly built home.

Designer Sandra L. Steiner rooted the room in nature, with Brazilian cherry flooring, teak and granite countertops, and tumbled marble at the hearth. This earthy mixture of natural materials and colors is balanced by soft ivory cabinets, finished with an overlay of chocolate glaze. Red tones in the speckled granite are echoed in the burgundy of the serving hutch.

The cabinet architecture creates a layered series of spaces that defines life in this kitchen. The main cooking station, with a professional range and double-arch detailing, is framed by a handsome mantelpiece with corbels carved in an acanthus leaf design. The arch motif continues over the cleanup station that opens to the wet bar and pantry. A third archway, built into the burgundy hutch, provides the kitchen with a view into the living room, which includes an impressive fieldstone fireplace. Two side-by-side islands complete the layout. The teak-topped prep station houses a microwave and additional storage below eye level, as well as one of the kitchen's three sinks. Its granite-topped companion is both a serving space and a back for the banquette for the pretty, round table.

The cabinets were designed in several contrasting patterns: beaded-inset, raised-panel doors in a variety sizes and shapes; glazed, illuminated cabinets and dish racks for display; and flat-panel drawer fronts. Next to the farm sink is an open cabinet with extendable towel bar. Some cabinets are set on feet while others sit flush on the floor. The respect for detail continues in the crown molding above the cabinets and in the treatment of the passage doors as well.

LEFT AND OPPOSITE The palette of maple, steel, and richly grained green, taupe, and crimson granite creates a serene yet cozy environment, shut off from the busy world outside.
Design: Stephen Chung

Carol wanted a quiet oasis. After interviewing several designers, she selected Stephen Chung to bring his elegant signature to her new apartment. The kitchen is just one manifestation of a unifying design concept that Chung applied to the entire project: He begins with function, but then allows it to evolve gently into abstract form. The concept is beautifully illustrated by the maple that extends beyond the kitchen cabinets, pivoting along the side wall to provide display niches, and then metamorphosing into a pure, geometric shape.

To enhance the purity of the design, electrical outlets were installed inside drawers and cabinets to allow all of the small appliances to be tucked out of sight, and even the clutter of hardware was eliminated by Chung's use of open rectangular recesses in lieu of traditional pulls.

Carol Lucas has been collecting pre-Columbian and African art for more than twenty years. Attracted to both the purity of the forms and the simple lives led by the artists who created them, Carol designed her home to have that same easy clarity. She wanted the loft, which is in a newly constructed "bridge building" between two old Boston warehouses, to "feel like an art gallery, to show the art, and to be a clean living environment with no clutter."

Nestled in a back corner, the kitchen gives Carol an expansive view through the front wall of windows that includes the old warehouse in which Carol operates her busy, noisy candle factory, cluttered with machinery and layered with wax on all the walls and floors.

"My incredible kitchen . . . the first thing you do when you walk in there is smile."

Working with an enthusiastic home owner who loves to have "something beautiful everywhere you look" and for whom a warm and welcoming feeling is the most important purpose of design, Mick De Giulio, along with interior designer Mary Ellen Henderson, created this elegant and thoroughly personal kitchen.

Graciously ensconced in four acres of flowery gardens, this kitchen composition begins in the pantry; continues through the main workroom, an interior vestibule, and a breakfast room; and culminates in an English conservatory. Designed within a unified architectural vision, these five independent spaces flow together gracefully, each adding a unique layer of function and aesthetic appeal.

A buttery glow from the integrated plaster walls and gentle striations of the yellow-and-biscuit-colored cabinetry shines through the adjoining spaces as the color palette quickly picks up momentum. Amber, burnished gold, and bronze tones are complemented by rich aubergine. Limestone and ceramic floors and granite counters in textured neutrals accentuate the reddish undertones of ebonized walnut and butternut cabinets in the main kitchen and vestibule.

The classic arch of the limestone structure over the kitchen window repeats at the hearth. The hood, despite its size and strength, sits lightly above the range. Below, a tightly set quilt of tiny, unglazed Jerusalem stone surrounds an arched recess of diagonally set glazed tiles of eggplant and brown. The wooden drawers flanking the range are recessed into frameworks of plaster, reinforcing a sense of architectural permanence.

A hardworking center island includes an ice maker, a dishwasher, willow storage baskets, and a row of undercounter stools, and features a deep stone sink with integrated drain board and custom cutting board.

Under a barrel vault in the narrow vestibule beyond, De Giulio inset a pair of raised-panel, hand-carved armoires.

One conceals the refrigerator; the second — a minikitchen for the guys — includes two microwave ovens, freezer drawers, and an ample supply of peanut butter and jelly. (Doors pivot away so that sandwich making is not impeded!) Between the armoires, a gilded aubergine cabinet is topped with a thick slab of cream-and-eggplant marble with a French *ovalo* corner. In the breakfast room beyond, a family table and lazy Susan were painted with a floral pattern in eggplant and amber, then topped with glass. A simply framed, flat-screen TV hangs above a sideboard, and six French country chairs complete the space. These rooms are filled with numerous details intended by De Giulio to reveal themselves over time, including several gentle references to the sun.

In the deceptively simple design shown here, architect Michael Gelick arranged the architectural elements to create a "receptacle" for the beautiful panoramic view of Lake Michigan just outside.

The mono-pitch roof angles up to draw in the light, which is then bounced off the modular, pewter-colored ceiling panels to reflect the ever-changing vista. Sky and water continuously define and redefine the forms and feeling of the room, hour by hour, season by season.

By the creative process of *elimination,* upper cabinets were replaced by walls of windows, further enhancing the continuity between interior and exterior spaces. When raised, the large art-glass window above the sink serves as a pass-through to the adjacent breakfast/family room, and also frames magnificent views of the great terrace, landscaped bluff, private beach, and lake. For privacy and sound control, its electrically powered retractable panels can be lowered during big parties, when the kitchen is bustling with caterers.

With the consistent repetition of natural materials in a neutral palette and a new, open flow of space, what was once a 1950s ranch house has been completely transformed.

Integrated with the 80' expanse of exterior glass wall to the east, this kitchen discretely camouflages all its modern equipment and high-tech function, graciously blending with the transparent and timeless architecture of the home and its environment.

RIGHT While his feelings were a bit bruised when a neighbor called his kitchen design "ugly," Joe asked his friends and readers to judge for themselves. Their responses indicate that Joe's kitchen is a total success.
Design: Joseph Holtzman

Nobody loves color, pattern, and texture — art and design — more than decorator/publisher Joseph Holtzman. His Manhattan apartment is vivaciously layered with artwork and other visual delights that range from classic to experimental. A visit to Joe's place is like a three-dimensional tour of his *Nest* magazine: 100 percent dazzle and fun.

Aching to resurface the drab and greasy walls of his cookie-cutter city kitchen, Joe collaborated with artist Pat O'Brien. The motto, fight song, and triumphal march to which they work is "When in doubt, paint it out!"

Now the small corridor space glistens within a rainbow world of donut shapes. The only architectural adjustment was the addition of the horizontal shelf above the cabinets that shows off Joe's rare collection of vintage ceramic strawberry shortcakes. The window was given the same treatment as the cabinetry, creating the effect of nouveau stained glass. The same delightful freedom is expressed in the task lights that move, wires and all, like fantastic mobiles when Joe opens the cupboards. The oriental rug — a formal touch — and color-coordinated doggie dish make life in this kitchen comfortable and convenient for Joe's standard poodle, Guido, and everyone else.

Final Thoughts

Our kitchens, so much at the center of our daily lives, reveal a lot about who we are. For many of the people I've spoken with — designers and home owners alike — kitchen stories are among their most treasured personal memories. Many (though certainly not all) of these memories seem to be set at a kitchen table . . . often the friendliest spot in the home.

When I think back over all the kitchens I've lived in, from the miniscule galley kitchen in the house trailer my parents owned when my father was in the Navy, to the kitchen in Ann Arbor that Richard and I shared when we were first married (in which we had two 10" TVs — one with picture but no sound, and one with sound but no picture), to our kitchen today, I realize that I've never had a kitchen I didn't love. There's always been a way to make each kitchen, whatever its limitations, work successfully.

Our kitchens tell the stories of who we are. They reflect our values and our dreams. And they remain, as ever, the best possible place to share the best of times with the people we love.

credits

COVER. design: Stuart Cohen & Julie Hacker Architects, Evanston, IL; Christine H. Bakalar Designs, Highland Park, IL; photograph: Paul Schlismann, Deerfield, IL; stylist: Linda Silbert; props: Taryn Kutchin; hair: Edwin Quiros; makeup: Stella Michail; wardrobe: Sue Bush

FRONT MATTER. p. I, design: Stuart Cohen & Julie Hacker Architects, Evanston, IL, and Christine H. Bakalar Designs, Highland Park, IL; photograph: Jon Miller © Hedrich-Blessing, Chicago, IL; p. 2, design: Jerrold Brim, Brim Consulting LLC Architects, Northbrook, IL; photograph: Anthony May Photography, Chicago, IL; p. 6, top row: (left) design: Bruce Bierman Design, Inc., New York, NY; photograph: Andrew Bordwin, New York, NY; (middle) design: Fu-Tung Cheng (with Milton Tong and Frank Lee), Cheng Design, Berkeley, CA; photograph: © Ching-Wei Jiang, Berkeley, CA; (right) design: Carrie Anne Deane, Kitchens by Deane, Inc., New Canaan, CT; photograph: Nancy Hill, Ridgefield, CT; middle row: (left) design: Marmol Radziner + Associates, AIA, Santa Monica, CA; photograph: Tim Street-Porter, Los Angeles, CA; (middle) design: Gerard Ciccarello, CKD, CBD, Covenant Kitchens & Baths, Inc., Westbrook, CT; photograph: © 2002jimfiora.com, Wallingford, CT; (right) design: Barbara Jacobs, FASID, Barbara Jacobs Interior Design, Los Gatos, CA; photograph: © 1996 Douglas A. Salin, San Francisco, CA; bottom row: (left) design: Jackie Brown, Olde World Cabinet Company, Winter Park, FL, and Marc-Michaels Interior Design, Inc., Winter Park, FL; photograph: © Kim Sargent, Palm Beach Gardens, FL; (middle) design: Fu-Tung Cheng (with Frank Lee), Cheng Design, Berkeley, CA; photograph: Matthew Millman, El Cerrito, CA; (right) design: Brininstool + Lynch, Chicago, IL; photograph: Christopher Barrett © Hedrich-Blessing, Chicago, IL

INTRODUCTION. p. 9, design: Adolfo Perez, Architect, Newton, MA; photograph: © Eric Roth, Topsfield, MA

PRELUDE. p. 10, design: Mick De Giulio, de Giulio kitchen design, inc., Wilmette, IL; photograph: Jon Miller © Hedrich-Blessing, Chicago, IL

PART ONE SECTION OPENER. design: Douglas Teiger, AIA, Abramson Teiger Architects, Culver City, CA; photograph: © John E. Linden, Woodland Hills, CA

CHAPTER ONE. p. 14, design: Thomas Richard Kelly, NorthShore Kitchens Plus, Inc., Marblehead, MA; photograph: Dan Walsh, Beverly, MA; p. 15, design: Deborah T. Lipner, Deborah T. Lipner, Ltd., Greenwich, CT; photograph: Durston Saylor, New York, NY; p. 16, design: Chip Webster, Chip Webster & Associates, Inc., Nantucket, MA; photograph: Jeffrey Allen Photography, Nantucket, MA; p. 17, design: Brininstool + Lynch, Chicago, IL; photograph: Padgett and Company, Chicago, IL; p. 18, design: Troy L. Adams, Studio Becker, West Hollywood, CA; photograph: Troy L. Adams, Los Angeles, CA; p. 19, design: Sura Malaga-Strachan, SRM Design Group, Inc., Holmdel, NJ; photograph: Rosemary Carroll, Doylestown, PA; pp. 20–21, design: Jackie Brown, Olde World Cabinet Company, Winter Park, FL, and Marc-Michaels Interior Design, Inc., Winter Park, FL; photographs: © Kim Sargent, Palm Beach Gardens, FL; pp. 22–23, design: Jean Stoffer, Jean Stoffer Design, Ltd., River Forest, IL; photographs: Robert Shimer © Hedrich-Blessing, Chicago, IL; p. 24, design: Emanuela Frattini Magnusson, EFM Design, New York, NY; photographs: Mario Carrieri, Milan, Italy; p. 25, (left) design: Joseph Groff, Principal, CCBG Architects, Inc., Phoenix, AZ; photograph: courtesy of CCBG Architects, Phoenix, AZ; (right) Barbara Jacobs, FASID, Barbara Jacobs Interior Design, Los Gatos, CA; photograph: © Russell MacMasters, San Francisco, CA; pp. 26–27, design: Ruhl Walker Architects, Inc. (Bradford C. Walker, AIA, and William T. Ruhl, AIA), Boston, MA; photographs: Glenn Daidone, Miami Beach, FL

CHAPTER TWO. pp. 28–29, design: Douglas Teiger, AIA, Abramson Teiger Architects, Culver City, CA; photographs: © John E. Linden, Woodland Hills, CA; p. 30, design: Brininstool + Lynch, Chicago, IL; photograph: Christopher Barrett © Hedrich-Blessing, Chicago, IL; p. 31, design: Sandra L. Steiner, CKD, Steiner & Houck, Inc., Columbia, PA; photograph: Peter Leach, Denver, PA; p. 32, design: Strittmatter Studios (John and Melia Strittmatter), Greenwich, CT; photograph: Michael Partenio, Danbury, CT; p. 33, (left) design: Dalia Tamari, Dalia Kitchen Design, Inc., Boston, MA; photograph: © Chalon UK Limited; (right) design: Cameron Snyder, CKD, Kitchen Concepts, Inc., Norwell, MA; photograph: John Ferrarone, Brookfield, MA; p. 34, design: Woodmeister Corp., Worcester, MA (with Anthony Catalfano Interiors, Boston, MA); photograph: Steve Vierra, Sandwich, MA; p. 35, (left) design: Emanuela Frattini Magnusson, EFM Design, New York, NY; photograph: Jürgen Frank, New York, NY; (right) design: Adolfo Perez, Architect, Newton, MA; photograph: Nick Wheeler, Weston, MA; p. 36, design: Fu-Tung Cheng (with Frank Lee), Cheng Design, Berkeley, CA; photograph: Matthew

Millman, El Cerrito, CA; p. 37, design: Colette and William Rodon Hornof, 2RZ Architecture, Inc., Chicago, IL; photograph: © Alan Shortall, Chicago, IL; p. 38, design: Foster Dale, Foster Dale Architects, Inc., Chicago, IL; photograph: Anthony May Photography, Chicago, IL; p. 39, design: Andre Rothblatt, AIA, Andre Rothblatt Architecture, San Francisco, CA; photograph: © Ken Gutmaker, San Francisco, CA; p. 40, design: Andre Rothblatt, AIA, Andre Rothblatt Architecture, San Francisco, CA; photograph: © Ken Gutmaker, San Francisco, CA; p. 41, design: Sally Cernik Weston, Weston Hewitson Architects, Inc., Hingham, MA; photograph: © 2002 Brian Vanden Brink, Photographer

CHAPTER THREE. pp. 42–43, design: Jack Murchie, AIA, and Marta Gazda Auskalnis, Schroeder Murchie Laya Associates, Ltd., Chicago, IL; photographs: Leslie Schwartz Photography, Chicago, IL; pp. 46 (right) and 47, design: Ashley Cole, Atria Studio, Chicago, IL; photographs: Tim Hobbs, Oak Park, IL

CHAPTER FOUR. pp. 50–51, design: Brininstool + Lynch, Chicago, IL; photographs: Christopher Barrett © Hedrich-Blessing, Chicago, IL; p. 52, design: Brininstool + Lynch, Chicago, IL; photograph: Padgett and Company, Chicago, IL; p. 53, design: Andre Rothblatt, AIA, Andre Rothblatt Architecture, San Francisco, CA; photograph: © Ken Gutmaker, San Francisco, CA; p. 54, design: Bailey Edward Design (Ellen Dickson, AIA, NCARB; Robin Whitehurst, AIA; Joakim Backstrom, AIA), Chicago, IL; photograph: Anthony May Photography, Chicago, IL; p. 55, (above) design: Lisa McCauley, McCauley Design — Kitchens, Barrington, IL; photograph: Robert Mauer Photography, Highland Park, IL; (below) design: Nancy Mullan, ASID, CKD, NDM Kitchens, New York, NY; photograph: Bill Holt, Seattle, WA; p. 56, design: Luna Design Group, Lynnfield, MA; photograph: Charles Mayer Photography, Concord, MA; p. 57, (above) design: Betty Torrell, Torrell Architects, Seattle, WA; photograph: R. Lauris Bitners, Seattle, WA; (below) design: Joan DesCombes, CKD, President, Architectural Artworks Incorporated, Winter Park, FL; photograph: Everett & Soulé, Altamonte Springs, FL; p. 59, design: Mick De Giulio, de Giulio kitchen design, inc., Wilmette, IL; photograph: Jon Miller © Hedrich-Blessing, Chicago, IL; p. 60, design: Nancy Mullan, ASID, CKD, NDM Kitchens, New York, NY; photograph: Bill Holt, Seattle, WA; p. 61, design: Rebecca Reynolds, The Kitchen Company, North Haven, CT; photograph: Olson Photographic LLC, Higganum, CT

CHAPTER FIVE. pp. 62–63, design: Kathy Jackson, J. Wheeler Ltd. and the Branch Cabinetry, Albuquerque, NM (with Ansaldi Shaw Design, Tucson, AZ); photographs: Kirk E. Gittings, Albuquerque, NM; pp. 64–65, design: Scott Himmel, Scott Himmel Architects, Chicago, IL, and Mick De Giulio, de Giulio kitchen design, inc., Wilmette, IL; photographs: Scott Frances, New York, NY; p. 66, design: Dianne Harsch, Emphasis Planning & Design, Del Mar, CA; photograph: Brett Drury Architectural Photography, Escondido, CA; p. 67, design: Barbara Houston, M. Arch. B.E.S., Houston + Associates, Vancouver, BC; photograph: Ron Hoffart, Surrey, BC; p. 68, (left) design: Mick De Giulio, de Giulio kitchen design, inc., Wilmette, IL; photograph: Paul Schlismann, Deerfield, IL; (right) design: Chip Webster, Chip Webster & Associates, Inc., Nantucket, MA; photograph: Peter Vanderwarker, West Newton, MA; p. 69, design: Erica Broberg, RA, AIA, Erica Broberg Architect, East Hampton, NY; photograph: © davidduncanlivingston.com, Mill Valley, CA; p. 70, design: Lisa Breznak, Lisa Breznak Decorative Arts, Peekskill, NY; photographs: Howard Goodman, Peekskill, NY; p. 71, design: Andre Rothblatt, AIA, Andre Rothblatt Architecture, San Francisco, CA; photographs: © Ken Gutmaker, San Francisco, CA; p. 72, (left) design: Jean Verbridge, ASID, IIDA, and Thaddeus Siemasko, AIA, Siemasko + Verbridge, Beverly, MA; photograph: Robert Benson, Hartford, CT; (right) design: Stephen A. Kinon, CKD, Ulrich, Inc., Ridgewood, NJ, and Fran Murphy, Fran Murphy and Associates, Saddle River, NJ; photograph: Phillip Ennis Photography, Bedford, NY; p. 73, (above) design: Beth Veillette, Hanford Cabinet & Woodworking, Inc., Old Saybrook, CT; photograph: J. R. Emmanuelli, Freehold, NJ; (below) design: Gioi Tran and Vernon Applegate, Applegate Tran Interiors, Inc., San Francisco, CA; photograph: Anna Dal Pino, Oakland, CA; p. 74, (above) design: Christine Julian, Julian Kitchen Design, Chicago, IL; photograph: kaskelphoto.com, Skokie, IL; (below) design: Betty Torrell, Torrell Architects, Seattle, WA; photograph: R. Lauris Bitners, Seattle, WA; p. 75, design: Joan DesCombes, CKD, President, Architectural Artworks Incorporated, Winter Park, FL; photograph: Everett & Soulé, Altamonte Springs, FL; p. 76, (above) design: Stuart Cohen & Julie Hacker Architects, Evanston, IL, Christine Julian, Julian Kitchen Design, Chicago, IL, and Stephanie Wohlner, Stephanie Wohlner Interior Designs, Highland Park, IL; photograph: Jon Miller © Hedrich-Blessing, Chicago, IL; (below) design: Mick De Giulio, de Giulio kitchen design, inc., Wilmette, IL; photograph: Jon Miller © Hedrich-Blessing, Chicago, IL; p. 77, (above) design and photograph: Jean Stoffer, Jean Stoffer Design, Ltd., River Forest, IL; (below) design: Stephen and Wendy Gardner, New York, NY; photograph: Wendy Gardner, New York, NY

CHAPTER SIX. p. 78, design: Nancy Mullan, ASID, CKD, NDM Kitchens, New York, NY; photograph: Phillip Ennis Photography, Bedford, NY; p. 79, design: Brininstool + Lynch, Chicago, IL; photograph: Padgett and Company, Chicago, IL; p. 80, (left) design: Nancy Mullan, ASID, CKD, NDM Kitchens, New York, NY; photograph: Bill Holt, Seattle, WA; (right) design: Brininstool + Lynch, Chicago, IL; photograph: Christopher Barrett © Hedrich-Blessing, Chicago, IL; p. 81, (left) design: Thomas Richard Kelly, NorthShore Kitchens Plus, Inc., Marblehead, MA; photograph: Dan Walsh, Beverly, MA; (right) design: Marmol Radziner + Associates, AIA, Santa Monica, CA; photograph: Tim Street-Porter, Los Angeles, CA; p. 82, (left) design: Fu-Tung Cheng (with Janet Szalay), Cheng Design, Berkeley, CA; photograph: Matthew Millman, El Cerrito, CA; (right) design: Stuart Cohen & Julie Hacker Architects, Evanston, IL; photograph: Nick Merrick © Hedrich-Blessing, Chicago, IL; p. 83, (left) design: Mary Douglas Drysdale, Drysdale, Inc., Washington, DC; photograph: Andrew D. Lautman, Washington, DC; (right) design: Bruce Bierman Design, Inc., New York, NY; photograph: Andrew Bordwin, New York, NY; p. 84, (left) design: Pamela Bytner, CKD, Bytner Design Associates, Clarkston, MI; photograph: © Beth Singer, Franklin, MI; (right) design: Jack Murchie, AIA, and Marta Gazda Auskalnis, Schroeder Murchie Laya Associates, Ltd., Chicago, IL; photograph: Leslie Schwartz Photography, Chicago, IL; p. 85, (left) design: Adolfo Perez, Architect, Newton, MA; photograph: Peter Vanderwarker, West Newton, MA; (right) design: Sally Cernik Weston, Weston Hewitson Architects, Inc., Hingham, MA; photograph: © Sam Gray, Boston, MA

CHAPTER SEVEN. (all) design: Clodagh, Clodagh Design International, New York, NY; photograph: Daniel Aubry, New York, NY; additional resources: National Kitchen + Bath Association (NKBA): (800) 843–6522; American Institute of Architects (AIA): (800) 242–3837; American Society of Interior Designers: www.interiors.org

PART TWO SECTION OPENER. design: Fu-Tung Cheng, Cheng Design, Berkeley, CA; photograph: © Richard Barnes, San Francisco, CA

CHAPTER EIGHT. p. 98, design: Chip Webster, Chip Webster & Associates, Inc., Nantucket, MA; photograph: Jeffrey Allen Photography, Nantucket, MA; p. 99, design: Joan DesCombes, CKD, President, Architectural Artworks Incorporated, Winter Park, FL; photograph: Everett & Soulé, Altamonte Springs, FL; p. 100, design: Lisa McCauley, McCauley Design — Kitchens, Barrington, IL; photographs: Paul Schlismann, Deerfield, IL; p. 101, (left) design: Mary Douglas Drysdale, Drysdale, Inc., Washington, DC; photograph: Andrew D. Lautman, Washington, DC; (right) design: Lisa McCauley, McCauley Design — Kitchens, Barrington, IL; photograph: Paul Schlismann, Deerfield, IL; p. 102, design: Cynthia S. Muni, Kitchens and Interiors, Northfield Center, OH, and Sandra R. Williams, Richfield, OH; photograph: Cyndee Duhon, Cuyahoga Falls, OH; p. 103, design: Stuart Cohen & Julie Hacker Architects, Evanston, IL, and Jennifer Morgenstern, Highland Park, IL; photograph: Jon Miller © Hedrich-Blessing, Chicago, IL; pp. 104–105, design: Yves-Claude, Yves-Claude I.D., Inc., New York, NY; photographs: Dusan Relgin, New York, NY; pp. 106–107, design: Joan DesCombes, CKD, President, Architectural Artworks Incorporated, Winter Park, FL; photographs: Everett & Soulé, Altamonte Springs, FL; pp. 108–109, design: Andre Rothblatt, AIA, Andre Rothblatt Architecture, San Francisco, CA; photographs: © Ken Gutmaker, San Francisco, CA; p. 110, design: Jean Verbridge, ASID, IIDA, and Thaddeus Siemasko, AIA, Siemasko + Verbridge, Beverly, MA; photograph: Avanti Studios, Boston, MA; p. 111, design: Joan DesCombes, CKD, President, Architectural Artworks Incorporated, Winter Park, FL; photograph: Everett & Soulé, Altamonte Springs, FL; pp. 112–113, design: Mark T. White, CKD, Kitchen Encounters, MTW Inc., Annapolis, MD; photographs: kaskelphoto.com, Skokie, IL

CHAPTER NINE. p. 114, design: Mick De Giulio, de Giulio kitchen design, inc., Wilmette, IL; photograph: Jon Miller © Hedrich-Blessing, Chicago, IL; p. 115, design: Marcus Gleysteen, AIA, Gleysteen Design LLC, Cambridge, MA; photograph: Richard Mandelkorn, Lincoln, MA; p. 116, design: Trevor D. Abramson, AIA, Abramson Teiger Architects, Culver City, CA; photograph: © John E. Linden, Woodland Hills, CA; p. 117, (left) design: Eric Owen Moss, Eric Owen Moss Architects, Culver City, CA; photograph: Scott Frances, New York, NY; (right) design: Thomas Richard Kelly, NorthShore Kitchens Plus, Inc., Marblehead, MA; photograph: Dan Walsh, Beverly, MA; p. 118, (above) design: Yves-Claude, Yves-Claude I.D., Inc., New York, NY; photograph: Dusan Relgin, New York, NY; (below) design: Kent Duckham, Duckham + McDougal Architects, Boston, MA; photograph: © Sam Gray, Boston, MA; p. 119, (left) design: Pasanella + Klein Stolzman + Berg Architects, P.C., New York, NY; photograph: © Paul Warchol, New York, NY; (right) design: O. Franco Nonahal, Kitchen Studio, Birmingham, MI; photograph: Beth Singer, Franklin, MI; p. 120, (left) design: Stuart Cohen & Julie Hacker Architects, Evanston, IL, and Jennifer Morgenstern, Highland Park, IL; photograph: Jon Miller © Hedrich-Blessing, Chicago, IL; (right) design: Cameron Snyder, CKD (with Gene Hester), Kitchen Concepts, Inc., Norwell, MA; photograph: John Ferrarone, Brookfield, MA; p. 121, (above) design: O. Franco Nonahal, Kitchen Studio, Birmingham, MI; photograph: Beth Singer, Franklin, MI; (below) design: Roger N. Goldstein, FAIA, Brookline, MA; photograph: Peter Vanderwarker, West Newton, MA; p. 122, design: Mark T. White, CKD, Kitchen Encounters, MTW Inc., Annapolis, MD; photograph: kaskelphoto.com, Skokie, IL; p. 123, (above) design: Gary and Marty

Matson, Metro Design, Columbia, SC; photograph: G. Matson Photo, Cola, SC; (below) design: Mojo Stumer Associates, Greenvale, NY; photograph: Jennifer Levy, New York, NY; p. 124, (left) design: Scott Salvator, Scott Salvator, Inc., New York, NY; photograph: Michael Hunter; (right: above and below) design: Adolfo Perez, Architect, Newton, MA; photographs: © Eric Roth, Topsfield, MA; p. 125, design: Fu-Tung Cheng (with Janet Szalay), Cheng Design, Berkeley, CA; photograph: Matthew Millman, El Cerrito, CA; pp. 126–127, design: Jean Verbridge, ASID, IIDA, Siemasko + Verbridge, Beverly, MA; photographs: Avanti Studios, Boston, MA; pp. 128–129, design: Marmol Radziner + Associates, AIA, Santa Monica, CA; photographs: Tim Street-Porter, Los Angeles, CA; pp. 130–131, design: Adolfo Perez, Architect, Newton, MA; photographs: Nick Wheeler, Weston, MA; pp. 132–133, design: Deborah H. Timmermann, ASID, Island House, Nantucket, MA; photographs: Jeffrey Allen Photography, Nantucket, MA

CHAPTER TEN. p. 134, design: Pete Giorgi, MCKBD, Giorgi Kitchens & Designs, Inc., Wilmington, DE, and Ellen Cheever, MCKBD, ASID, Wilmington, DE; photograph: Bob McClain, McClain Imagery, Wilmington, DE; p. 135, design: Adolfo Perez, Architect, Newton, MA; photograph: Peter Vanderwarker, West Newton, MA; p. 136, (left) design: Stuart Cohen & Julie Hacker Architects, Evanston, IL, and Christine H. Bakalar Designs, Highland Park, IL; photograph: Jon Miller © Hedrich-Blessing, Chicago, IL; (right) design: Joan DesCombes, CKD, President, Architectural Artworks Incorporated, Winter Park, FL; photograph: Everett & Soulé, Altamonte Springs, FL; p. 137, design: Marmol Radziner + Associates, AIA, Santa Monica, CA; photograph: Tim Street-Porter, Los Angeles, CA; p. 138, design: Ricki Brown, CKD, Modern Kitchen Center, Glenwood Springs, CO; photograph: Jay Curtis, Denver, CO; p. 140, design: Maxine Snider, Maxine Snider, Inc., Chicago, IL; photograph: Hedrich-Blessing, Chicago, IL; p. 141, design: Gerard Ciccarello, CKD, CBD, Covenant Kitchens & Baths, Inc., Westbrook, CT; photographs: © 2002 jimfiora.com, Wallingford, CT; pp. 142–143, design: Carrie Anne Deane, Kitchens by Deane, Inc., New Canaan, CT; photographs: Nancy Hill, Ridgefield, CT; pp. 144–145, design: John C. Senhauser, FAIA, John Senhauser Architects, Cincinnati, OH; photographs: Corson Hirschfeld, Cincinnati, OH; pp. 146–147, design: Joan DesCombes, CKD, President, Architectural Artworks Incorporated, Winter Park, FL; photographs: Everett & Soulé, Altamonte Springs, FL; pp. 148–149, design: Marmol Radziner + Associates, AIA, Santa Monica, CA; photographs: Benny Chan-fotoworks, Los Angeles, CA; pp. 150–151, design: William T. Ruhl, AIA, and Bradford C. Walker, AIA, Ruhl Walker Architects, Inc., Boston, MA; photographs: Jordi Miralles, Barcelona, Spain

CHAPTER ELEVEN. pp. 152–153, design: Bruce Bierman Design, Inc., New York, NY; photographs: Andrew Bordwin, New York, NY; p. 154, design: C. Larry Horne, ASID, Horne International Designs, Inc., Bethesda, MD, and Eric Lieberknecht, Rutt of D.C., Washington, DC; photograph: John Umberger, Real Images, Inc., Jasper, GA; p. 155, (above) design: Emanuela Frattini Magnusson, EFM Design, New York, NY; photograph: Gionata Xerra, Milan, Italy; (below) design: Fu-Tung Cheng (with Frank Lee), Cheng Design, Berkeley, CA; photograph: Matthew Millman, El Cerrito, CA; p. 156, design: Ricki Brown, CKD, Modern Kitchen Center, Glenwood Springs, CO; photograph: Jay Curtis, Denver, CO; p. 157, (above) design: Fu-Tung Cheng (with Janet Szalay), Cheng Design, Berkeley, CA; photograph: © Richard Barnes, San Francisco, CA; (below) design: Beverly A. Alig, CKD, Kitchen Encounters, MTW Inc., Annapolis, MD; photograph: Ray Studios, Inc., Baltimore, MD; p. 158, design: Ricki Brown, CKD, Modern Kitchen Center, Glenwood Springs, CO; photograph: Jay Curtis, Denver, CO; pp. 160–161, design: Barbara Jacobs, FASID, Barbara Jacobs Interior Design, Los Gatos, CA; photographs: © Russell MacMasters, San Francisco, CA; pp. 162–163, design: Fu-Tung Cheng, Cheng Design, Berkeley, CA; photographs: © Richard Barnes, San Francisco, CA; p. 164, design: Nancy Mullan, ASID, CKD, NDM Kitchens, New York, NY; photographs: Steven Mays, New York, NY; p. 165, design: Barbara Jacobs, FASID, Barbara Jacobs Interior Design, Los Gatos, CA; photographs: © 1996 by Douglas A. Salin, San Francisco, CA; pp. 166–167, design: Ricki Brown, CKD, Modern Kitchen Center, Glenwood Springs, CO; photographs: Jay Curtis, Denver, CO

CHAPTER TWELVE. pp. 168–171, design: Fu-Tung Cheng (with Milton Tong and Frank Lee), Cheng Design, Berkeley, CA; photographs: © Ching-Wei Jiang, Berkeley, CA; pp. 172–173, design: Brininstool + Lynch, Chicago, IL; photographs: Christopher Barrett © Hedrich-Blessing, Chicago, IL; pp. 174–175, design: Jackie Brown, Olde World Cabinet Company, Winter Park, FL, and Marc-Michaels Interior Design, Inc., Winter Park, FL; photographs: Kim Sargent, Palm Beach Gardens, FL; pp. 176–177, design: Betty Torrell, Torrell Architects, Seattle, WA; photographs: R. Lauris Bitners, Seattle, WA; pp. 178–179, design: Sandra L. Steiner, CKD, Steiner & Houck, Inc., Columbia, PA; photographs: Peter Leach, Denver, PA; pp. 180–181, design: Stephen Chung, Architect, mod. A, Boston, MA; photographs: Stephen Lee, Boston, MA; pp. 182–183, design: Mick De Giulio, de Giulio kitchen design, inc., Wilmette, IL, and Mary Ellen Henderson, Henderson Homes, Inc., Libertyville, IL; photographs: Paul Schlismann, Deerfield, IL; pp. 184–185, design: Michael Gelick, Gelick Associates, Inc., Chicago, IL; photographs: kaskelphoto.com, Skokie, IL; p. 186, design: Joseph Holtzman, New York, NY; photograph: Jason Schmidt, New York, NY

index

r

recycling bins, 139
resale value, 20, 24–25, 159
restraint, 28, 40
rooms, transitions between, 159

s

scale, 28, 38
sculpture, kitchens as, 37
seating areas, 78–85, 139
senses, using, 78
shelves, open, 58, 159
sight lines, 140, 159
sink:
    dry, 102
    placement of, 139
sizes, standard, 56
skylight, 120, 123, 154, 171
    faux, 24, 123, 172
soffit, 46
space:
    availability of, 20
    configuration of existing, 137
    corner, 140
    enlarging, 23, 116
    illusion of, 120
    and light, 114–33
    optimum use of, 56
    questions about, 48–49
steam, cooking with, 102
storage, questions about, 49
stove elements:
    modular, 102
    water-based, 102
stoves, professional caliber, 16, 159
style, 152–67
    Arts and Crafts, 161
    Asian-influenced, 74
    choosing, 78–85
    elements of, 159
    French country, 31, 154, 178–79
    Japanese, 172
    pueblo deco, 62–63
    Victorian, 22

t

tansu chests, 165
tape recorder, 44
texture, 28, 32–33
    variation in, 46
    white-on-white, 82
tool kit, 44–45
transoms, 127
triangle, kitchen, 26, 134

u

universal design, 112
Usonian house, 144

v

veneers, 56
ventilation:
    ductless, 159
    hoods for, 166–67, 171, 183
Victorian kitchen, 22
vision:
    developing a, 16–23,
    trusting your, 26
    See also dreams

w

wallpaper border, 68
walls:
    eliminating, 118
    of windows, 126–27, 185
warming drawer, 102
wet bar, 101, 145, 178
wheelchair accessibility, 102, 112, 140
wheels, uses for, 138
whites, multiple, 164
windows, 120
    clerestory, 11, 121
    walls of, 126–27, 185
workstations, multiple, 102, 109, 112, 136, 137
Wright, Frank Lloyd, 16, 144, 163